Praise for *The Mas*

"Once again, Lance Hahn presents a provocative and captivating discourse that is essential toward experiencing lives of vitality and fulfillment. *The Master's Mind* gives simple yet sacred definition to what has been captured through the redemptive and complete work of Jesus Christ. The enemies of our souls have been identified and defeated. Therefore, Lance Hahn *masterfully* leads us in walking out this victory through practical application and with unapologetic celebration. Read and be blessed."

—PARNELL M. LOVELACE JR., MSW, DMIN
LOVELACE LEADERSHIP CONNECTION

"In *The Master's Mind*, Lance Hahn has tackled one of the most foundational and important elements of Christian maturity, though one of the least talked about: how to bring every thought captive to Christ. This book reminds us all that we don't have to live as victims to our dysfunctions, temptations, and addictions, but as more than conquerors. Let this book empower you to transform your thought life in the image of our creator, the one who has surpassingly more for you than you can imagine or comprehend."

—REV. SAMUEL RODRIGUEZ
PRESIDENT OF THE NATIONAL HISPANIC
CHRISTIAN LEADERSHIP CONFERENCE

"Lance Hahn's second breakthrough book, *The Master's Mind*, goes full speed and without apology into the paradox and pain of mental well-being. In extraordinarily practical language, Lance explains the vast difference between a 'better' mind and a 'new' mind—the mind of the Master. This is a home run and much needed."

—SCOTT HAGAN
PRESIDENT, NORTH CENTRAL UNIVERSITY

"It is said in football that whoever controls the line of scrimmage will win the game. . . . My friend Lance Hahn has produced a timely yet needed book on getting victory in creation's 'line of scrimmage,' aka the mind. This book is a bit of a throwback to the early discipleship, Word-based classics that I cut my teeth on and were significant in my spiritual formation. . . . I recommend this book to all who want to walk in the fullness of what the Father had in mind when he created them."

—SEAN SMITH

AUTHOR, *I AM YOUR SIGN* AND *PROPHETIC EVANGELISM*

"I am so excited for this book. It is timely and very needed in our culture. The quest for identity is a natural one but one I believe is fraught with danger if we do not seek it from our creator. Our world, as well as the enemy of our soul, is constantly shouting out false identities that will lead us heart ache and misery. The question 'who am I?' should drive us into the arms of our loving heavenly Father. Lance's new book helps to do just that. Read it. Be encouraged. I was!"

—JENNY WILLIAMSON

FOUNDER/CEO, COURAGE WORLDWIDE, INC.

"Spoiler alert: this book reveals reality in clear fashion. We live in a world of startling paradoxes. None of those paradoxes is more startling or consistently enveloping of the human condition than that of our personal identity. My friend Lance Hahn has written beautifully in *The Master's Mind* about both the very real struggle and the paradoxical pathway to victory. This book will help you establish your identity, empower your daily life, and encourage your heart that you are not alone."

—JOHN JACKSON

PRESIDENT, WILLIAM JESSUP UNIVERSITY

AUTHOR AND SPEAKER

"The Bible is clear that transformation happens when our minds are renewed. It is in the battleground of the mind that we must gain victory if we are to walk out the fullness that is available to us through the power of the Holy Spirit. For so many believers there is a nagging feeling that there is more than what they have experienced in their walk with God, and they are right. God has destined us to live healthy and victorious lives, but for many of us that life feels out of reach. Lance Hahn addresses this in *The Master's Mind*. I encourage those who have a passion to fully understand who they are in Christ and a desire to see their minds renewed to read this book and see that a transformed life is their inheritance in Christ."

—BANNING LIEBSCHER
JESUS CULTURE FOUNDER AND PASTOR
AUTHOR, *ROOTED: THE HIDDEN PLACES WHERE GOD DEVELOPS YOU*

"'What were you thinking?' Those are the exact words my mom asked me every time I got in trouble (which was a lot). Maybe it's because she knew my actions were enslaved to the thoughts behind the behaviors. *The Master's Mind* helps us rethink our thinking, taking us on a journey of letting the Master master our minds."

—JONATHAN McKEE
AUTHOR, *IF I HAD A PARENTING DO OVER*
AND *THE TEEN'S GUIDE TO SOCIAL MEDIA AND MOBILE DEVICES*

"What do you think of how you think? Or have you thought about how you think? Lance Hahn has. He thinks about his own mind. He has thought about our minds. And he has thought about what the Scriptures say about our minds and how we think. This is captivating thinking—which is the point."

—BRAD FRANKLIN
SENIOR PASTOR, LAKESIDE CHURCH, FOLSOM, CA

"Your thoughts determine who you are and where you're headed. In Lance Hahn's latest book, *The Master's Mind*, you will discover how God can transform you into a new person when you let Him change the way you think (Romans 12:2). Get ready to grow in your understanding of having the 'mind of Christ' and how it affects every part of your life!"

—PERRY KALLEVIG
LEAD PASTOR, HARVEST CHURCH, ELK GROVE, CA

"In his most recent book, *The Master's Mind*, pastor Lance Hahn clearly lays out the struggle for our minds and then proceeds with the solution of how to master them and regain our identities by following specific biblical principles. Whether you struggle with temptation, addiction, or dysfunction, or simply need more discipline in order to have a balanced life, this book is certain to give you a fresh outlook and fill your soul with hope and faith toward freedom and a more productive life."

—DON AND CHRISTA PROCTOR
IMPACT CHURCH ROSEVILLE / CITY PASTORS SACRAMENTO

"In *The Master's Mind*, Lance Hahn does a phenomenal job addressing the source problems of our fear, anxieties, and spiritual struggles, in a way that is accessible, relatable, and incredibly powerful. May we all have ears to hear and the faith to act."

—RYAN MACDIARMID
LEAD PASTOR, CREEKSIDE CHURCH, ROCKLIN, CA

"'A war lost in the mind is lost!' In this powerful work, Lance masterfully expounds upon this principle to show us how to build up our mental toughness and spiritual swagger by taking on the mind of Christ. This book is a must-read for people seeking to overcome the limiting thoughts and beliefs that are causing them not to live new, healthy, and whole lives. Enough is enough! It's time to win the battle of your mind by learning how to take on the Master's Mind!"

—DR. TECOY PORTER SR.
SENIOR PASTOR, GENESIS CHURCH, SACRAMENTO, CA
AUTHOR, *FAITH TO INNOVATE: 21ST CENTURY TOOLS & STRATEGIES FOR LEADERSHIP TRANSFORMATION*

The Master's Mind

Also by Lance Hahn

How to Live in Fear: Mastering the Art of Freaking Out

The Master's Mind

The Art of Reshaping Your Thoughts

Lance Hahn

W PUBLISHING GROUP

AN IMPRINT OF THOMAS NELSON

Published in Nashville, Tennessee, by W Publishing, an imprint of Thomas Nelson.

Author is represented by the literary agency of Alive Communications, Inc., 7680 Goddard Street, Suite 200, Colorado Springs, CO 80920, www.alivecommunications.com.

Thomas Nelson titles may be purchased in bulk for educational, business, fundraising, or sales promotional use. For information, please e-mail SpecialMarkets@ThomasNelson.com.

ISBN 978-0-7180-3543-3 (SC)
ISBN 978-0-7180-3859-5 (eBook)

Library of Congress Cataloging-in-Publication Data
Library of Congress Control Number: 2017939572

Printed in the United States of America

17 18 19 20 21   LSC   10 9 8 7 6 5 4 3 2 1

*To the Father of Lights, the personal and powerful
Holy Spirit, and to Jesus Christ, my hero.*

*To my beautiful wife and my incredible daughters, who are
the greatest gifts that God has given me outside of salvation.*

*To Bridgeway Christian Church, the precious
stewardship entrusted to me by our Savior.*

*To the millions trying to get their thought lives
in order and wondering if they are the only
ones struggling: #YouAreNotAlone.*

Contents

Foreword

A while back my wife, Carol, and I took our daughters to Germany to visit our son at Bible school. While he was in class, we took a day trip down to the first Nazi concentration camp— Dachau. By the end of the war, more than thirty-two thousand Jews and other political prisoners were brutally slaughtered there.

We walked under the haunting "welcome" sign that said "Work Will Set You Free," then spent the day in those stark, thoroughly depressing grounds. Nobody says much as they're touring. The dreariness of the day simply underscored the blanket of somberness that descended on us. There was no laughter, no joy in that whole compound.

We listened to the recorded tour as we walked into rooms where gruesome experiments were conducted. We walked into gas chambers, into places where people were hung, into barracks where people were stacked on top of each other, into shower rooms where people were killed.

As snow flurries swirled around me, I stood in the middle of Dachau and thought, *What do you learn from this?*

What I learned was this: *ideas have consequences.* The saying "What you believe doesn't matter as long as you're sincere" could not be further from the truth. The Nazis believed they were a superior race. They believed they were justified in doing what they did to people. The Holocaust was the result of *ideas* they believed.

Forty years of Christian leadership, twenty-eight years of parenting, and one trip to Dachau have strengthened three core convictions for me, and here they are:

> Nobody *lives* well—until they think well.
> Nobody *loves* well—until they think well.
> Nobody *leads* well—until they think well.

The reason so many people are not living, loving, or leading well is because very few people are teaching people to think well!

Welcome to *The Master's Mind*! There are two reasons that I am excited you are about to read this book.

First, you have just picked up a book with the power to change your life!

I believe that all life change begins by changing the way we think.

So did the Apostle Paul, which is why he penned the following: "Do not conform any longer to the pattern of this world, but *be transformed by the renewing of your mind*" (Rom. 12:2 NIV).

The key to changing your life is to change the way you think. John Maxwell explains it best when he describes the five steps to transformational change:

1. When you change your **thinking**, you change your **beliefs**.
2. When you change your **beliefs**, you change your **expectations**.
3. When you change your **expectations**, you change your **attitude**.
4. When you change your **attitude**, you change your **behavior**.
5. When you change your **behavior**, you change your **life!**[1]

So all change starts in your thought life. Scripture says, "As [a man] thinks in his heart, so is he" (Prov. 23:7 NKJV).

Secondly, you have just picked up a book written by someone who lives what he writes!

For over a decade I have had a front-row seat to see Lance grow as a pastor and as a leader. Lance is a God-honoring pastor who *means* what he says in the pulpit and *lives* what he says outside it!

The Master's Mind is not a sterile book written from an ivory tower but is Lance spilling out the practical and essential steps that God has used to strengthen his life—which has led to the blessing of God on his ministry, marriage, and family.

And isn't that what we all want? Aren't we all hoping for God's blessing on our lives? Aren't we all looking for the type of power to overcome temptation? Aren't we all looking for a source of strength to help us bounce back from discouragement and live God-honoring lives?

As I read Lance's new book I thought, *Perfect timing*. American churches are now packed with people who need to get their fire back, get their hopes back up, and get their lives back on track.

Some books are must-reads. This book is a must-practice. *The Master's Mind* will help energize and equip Christians to live thriving lives and recapture the passion and power present in the early church and absent in the American church.

What's at stake? Everything! Every community needs Christians that live well. Every church needs people who lead well. Every family needs parents who love well. My prayer is that God will use this book to get his people back to basing their lives on *truth* instead of *trends*!

Ray Johnston
President, Thrive Communications
Pastor, Bayside Church

Introduction

What we think and believe determines who we are.

We are a mess.

We are insecure, defensive, lonely, empty, fearful, depressed, self-absorbed, dysfunctional, angry, and confused.

That's not what God has in mind for us.

In fact, the Master has a whole different list of attributes in mind for us: hope, strength, beauty, joy, love, creativity, freedom, power, peace, patience, goodness, laughter, organization, effectiveness, and purpose.

So what went wrong? How did we move so far from God's intentions?

We lost our identities in our sin. We've become unanchored and therefore tossed about on the sea of a million influences, none of which is our Master's heart or mind.

Between the flesh, the world, and the Devil, we don't know what to think, and, therefore, our lives are filled with hurt, pain, and regret. Someone is running the show in our minds, and it's not us—at least not the real us—nor is it the real owner.

Jesus is not okay with this. He died to save us from our sins and set us free. He made a way for our souls to be rescued from our enemies. He bought the territory of our minds and planted His flag on holy ground.

It's time for us to get angry enough to take back control of our minds, to master them and bring them back in alignment with the Master's will.

It's time to return to the Master's Mind.

> For the weapons of our warfare are not of the flesh but have *divine power to destroy strongholds. We destroy arguments and every lofty opinion raised against the knowledge of God*, and *take every thought captive to obey Christ.* (2 Cor. 10:4–5)

Chapter 1

The One Thing

In 1991, MGM studios released a film called *City Slickers*, starring Billy Crystal and Jack Palance. Billy's character, Mitch Robbins, and his two friends are going through a midlife identity crisis, so they think it's a good idea to join a dude ranch for two weeks and drive cattle from New Mexico to Colorado. Upon their arrival, they meet a crusty old cowboy named Curly (played by Palance), who seems to have his life figured out in its simplest form. As they ride along, Mitch has this conversation with Curly:

"Do you know what the secret of life is?" Curly asks in his gravelly voice.

"No, what?" Mitch replies.

"This." He holds up his index finger.

"Your finger?"

"One thing. Just one thing. You stick to that and everything else [doesn't matter]."[1]

How easy would life be if we could boil all of our situations down to *one thing*? Is that even possible? Oddly enough, sometimes it is.

In approximately AD 31, Jesus Christ of Nazareth was asked the seemingly impossible question: "What is the greatest commandment of God?"² Jesus was asked to cut through hundreds—some would argue thousands—of rules and regulations in traditional, orthodox Judaism and name the one thing that God the Father wanted most. Jesus simply replied, "Love the Lord your God with all your heart, mind, soul, and strength." The point was clear: if we do that, all else falls in line.

I'm not as brilliant as Jesus nor even as sharp as Curly, but I do know this: all the internal struggles we face every day—the questions of identity, the problems with temptation, the struggles with sin and doubt and fear—are connected to the way we think. Our minds are our "one thing." If we can master our minds and bring our thoughts into alignment with the Lord's will and perspective, the rest of our lives will follow suit.

I wonder how many of us fully understand the power of thoughts. Do we realize that what we think, we will ultimately do? There is no action that is not preceded by a thought. The human body is designed with a command center called the brain, and every system takes its control from that center. If we want to bring change to our lives—and who doesn't?—we must master things here first.

What's the Big Deal?

Why in the world would you want to read a book about changing your thoughts?

Because thoughts affect everything.

Most of us consider ourselves good people who mean well. Some of us even think our lives look fairly organized, but upon closer inspection—dear Lord! Deep down we are full of contradictions and sin, despite our best efforts. We can't even follow a diet and exercise program, much less grapple with crippling depression or anxiety. Every time we think we have things together, we do something shockingly selfish. Just when we think we have a bad habit under control, it breaks out again. The more we try to be humble, the more our ugly pride is revealed. For those of us who are Christians, we read the Bible and see that the standard God set for our lives is the life of Jesus—and we feel hopeless. But are we?

Absolutely not.

God made a way for us to live healthy and whole, and it doesn't have to be this way.

So much of our challenge is that we don't know who we are or why we are here. A healthy identity is the foundation for a right mind-set and victorious living. Praise the Lord that He has told us who He is, who we are in light of Him, and what we have been placed on this earth to do.

God does the heavy lifting. He does the rescuing and the saving. He does the deep-down transformation. Our job is to steward what He has given us. It's our responsibility to manage our bodies and our minds and to let Him make the changes we truly need. That's never going to happen if we don't do some serious work on our thoughts.

The Power of the Mind

What we think determines our actions. Even our emotions are secondary to our thoughts. We do good things because we think good things. We do bad things because we think bad things. Every great work and positive revolution in history has happened because men and women were inspired and then set their minds to carry the work to completion. Martin Luther King Jr. determined that he would not rest until all people were viewed as God intended— equal. Mother Teresa determined that the poor would not be forgotten. Our Lord Jesus Christ walked His entire life on earth with a focus on completely obeying His heavenly Father, including the determination to end up on the cross to save us from our sins, as we see in this passage from Luke: "When the days drew near for him to be taken up, he set his face to go to Jerusalem" (9:51).

Our thoughts drive our lives, both for good and for evil.

Yet it's not just a single poignant decision that determines our life paths. Life isn't that simple. A series of choices determines what today and tomorrow will hold. These decisions come from the contents of our minds, which are sometimes filled with truth and sometimes filled with error. The worst decisions of our pasts came from operating off a faulty premise.

The Bible tells us of an ancient, high-ranking official who made a personal choice that would dictate the rest of his life and effectiveness. His name was Naaman, and he was a Syrian army commander who had leprosy, a terrible skin disease. Knowing that he was desperate for healing, his little servant girl told him of a prophet in Israel who could heal him by God's power. Figuring that it was worth a shot, Naaman went to see the prophet Elisha. Elisha sent a messenger to tell Naaman that he would be healed if he washed seven times in the Jordan River.

Naaman was furious. First, he was insulted that the prophet didn't greet him personally. Second, he knew that the Jordan River in that area was less than appealing. Third, he thought the healing should be easier than that. He believed that the prophet was simply going to "call upon the name of the LORD his God, and wave his hand over the place and cure" him (2 Kings 5:11). When things didn't go the way he thought they should, he stormed off in a rage.

His attendants hurried after him and convinced him to reconsider. Sure, washing seven times was unorthodox, but what if it could heal him? Was it really so bad to wash in a river? Why not give it a try?

He relented—and came out healed from leprosy.

Naaman's false assumptions, ignorant thoughts, and prideful

heart almost cost him his healing. What are we believing today that is keeping us from God's best?

Our Journey Begins with a Thought

We've established that our thoughts determine our actions. But let's go one step even further back: what we believe—about God, about ourselves, about the world around us—determines what we think. Deep within each of our psyches is a belief system, a worldview, a lens through which we see life. From that mind-set comes the vast majority of our thoughts, and these thoughts will not change unless our belief systems change. We can't modify them easily; the truth is that the only way to monkey around in a belief system is through introducing new or healthier thoughts. Most of us cannot separate our beliefs from our thoughts (in fact, I will use those terms interchangeably), and only God can change our natures. So I'm going to focus on how to shape, change, and restore healthy thoughts into our minds so that our lives might align more closely with God's design.

Everything begins somewhere. Things don't just happen without cause. Every trail of bread crumbs starts with a single crumb. There's an origin, a starting point. For our purposes, that's a thought.

It's true of God: Isaiah 14:24 tells us, "The LORD of hosts has sworn: 'As I have planned, so shall it be, and as I have purposed, so shall it stand.'" God's plans precede His actions. Before God spoke the universe into being or said, "Let there be light" (Gen. 1:3), He thought about it first. The Bible is full of references to God saying that the events of history were in accordance with His plan all along:

> And he made from one man every nation of mankind to live on all the face of the earth, having determined allotted periods and the boundaries of their dwelling place. (Acts 17:26)

And we know that for those who love God all things work together for good, for those who are called according to his purpose. For those whom he foreknew he also predestined to be conformed to the image of his Son, in order that he might be the firstborn among many brothers. And those whom he predestined he also called, and those whom he called he also justified, and those whom he justified he also glorified. (Rom. 8:28–30; cf. Eph. 1:3–14; 2 Tim. 1:9–10; Judg. 14:4; Prov. 16:9, 33)

It's true for Good Guys: Before the New York firefighters and police officers ran into the collapsing Twin Towers on the fateful day of 9/11, they thought about it. Some would say they operated on instinct, but instinct is only habitual, deep-seated thought patterns. Their heroic choice to risk their lives to protect others from a burning building was the result of truly stunning thoughts: *My job is to rescue others and put them before myself. I will not let fear dictate my response. I have come to help, and that is what I will do. I won't leave until the last person is out.*

And it's true for Bad Guys: Before they ended up on the news, they committed the crime. Before they committed the crime, they thought about it. Whether it's a serial killer operating off the mindset that he has the right to harm another person or a racist who deems one group of people more valuable than another, whether the crime was premeditated or done in the heat of the moment, actions follow worldviews.

It's true for everyone: we all make decisions first in our minds before our bodies carry them out.

The Control Room

A number of years back, my wife and I were watching a submarine war movie. Every time the captain left the command room, he would say to the next guy in charge, "You have the conn." This phrase originated in the nineteenth century, when warships had "conning towers." When the captain of a ship says it, he means that his first mate is in charge of directing the ship while he is gone.

Just like every ship has a command room, so too do our bodies. Our minds are the command centers of our worlds. You can think of them like the Great and Powerful Oz, the guy behind the curtain who runs the show. They're where the magic happens and all the strings are being pulled. Therefore, if you have an adjustment to make, it seems practical to make it there first.

As often as we use the phrase "our hearts" when referring to emotion, the truth is that all of our thought processes emanate from the brain. The Bible says it this way—and as you read, remember to substitute the poetic *heart* with the real *mind*:

> "The good person *out of the good treasure of his heart* produces good, and the evil person *out of his evil treasure* produces evil, for *out of the abundance of the heart* his mouth speaks." (Luke 6:45)

> "But what comes out of the mouth proceeds from the heart, and this defiles a person. For *out of the heart* come evil thoughts, murder, adultery, sexual immorality, theft, false witness, slander. These are what defile a person." (Matt. 15:18–20)

Both of these quotes come from Jesus Christ of Nazareth, who was explaining that our characters and beliefs determine the lives we live. He was reacting to the religious leaders of His day who looked perfect and holy on the outside but were wicked and selfish on the inside. They thought that if they did enough religious activity and avoided obvious evil choices, they would be truly good people. Christ spent a large portion of His ministry exposing the hypocrisy of this line of thinking. Doing one thing on the outside doesn't make up for thinking another on the inside.

These passages make it clear that we can't fake it. What's inside our minds will spill over into our words and actions.

Identity, Worldview, and Reality

What makes this idea so revolutionary is that most of us spend our energy trying to shape our lives through our actions and behaviors. We see something wrong in how we are living and want to change it, so we try to merely stop doing the corresponding bad behavior. As well-intentioned as that may be, it's largely ineffective. Foolishly, we catapult over the root of the issue and start hacking at branches, only to be surprised when the branches grow back. When it comes to morality, we try to be nice people. When it comes to ethics, we try to do right things. And when it comes to matters of faith, we spend the majority of our energy on sin management, completely avoiding the core issues. We'll never experience transformation until we address the thoughts at the root of our problems.

What we believe ourselves to be—our *identities*—directly affects how we act. If we believe we are valuable, we will care for ourselves. If we don't, we'll put little thought into what happens to us. If we believe we are safe, we will have less anxiety. If we don't, we'll be fear-ridden. If we believe there is a God, our lives will reflect our faith. If we don't, then ultimately nothing will have meaning.

Our identities and our worldviews combine to create the perceived realities that our command centers (brains) are trying to navigate. What's ironic is that none of our perceived realities are correct, because none of us are dealing with all the facts. How we think the world works and our role within it are significantly fabricated. We live in fake worlds.

We view our realities through the knowledge and experiences we've accumulated. Every moment we add and subtract from them—sometimes on purpose, and sometimes by accident or by force. Nevertheless, we are missing countless facts that would significantly alter our worldview if we knew them.

Consider the young, beautiful, and vibrant twentysomething woman who is in a relationship with an abusive and overbearing boyfriend. Everyone on the outside sees her relationship one way, but she thinks about it differently. She is trapped into thinking that what is happening to her is acceptable. She may not like it or think it's right, but somehow her identity and worldview allow for it to continue.

She was shaped into thinking that she didn't deserve better. Perhaps her father abused her or treated her with disdain. Perhaps her mother lived in competition with her or acted out of pure self-ishness. Perhaps she fell into a group of friends that led her down a road of addiction, and her connection to this man has nothing to do with love and friendship but everything to do with mutual codependency. Every belief led to a decision, and every decision led to an action.

But what if she knew that Jesus thought she was valuable enough to die for? What if she knew that young women are supposed to be treated with respect, and that it's never okay for a man to strike a woman? What if she had been taught self-respect and a healthy identity early on? Would that not have changed her life?

What we think affects who we are.

What's at Stake?

A war lost in the mind is lost. Bad thinking is dangerous. Just as a wartime strategy based on faulty intelligence is a potential disaster, so too is an untrained and disorderly mind. Or, more subtly, wrong thinking can keep us ineffective, wasting time on things that aren't important instead of living the lives God has for us. Victory and defeat can happen between our ears.

Right thinking is a big deal. In fact, it's *the* deal.

Paul wrote in Romans about the distorted thinking common to humans—and the consequences it brings. Since our sin nature is rooted in how we think, our thoughts continue to be the primary block between us and God. Despite God's continual attempts to reveal Himself and His heart for mankind, He has been rejected at every turn. He desperately wants to renew our minds and align them with His, but we, as humans, resist Him every step of the way.

> For the wrath of God is revealed from heaven against all ungodliness and unrighteousness of men, *who by their unrighteousness suppress the truth. For what can be known about God is plain to them,* because God has shown it to them. For his invisible attributes, namely, his eternal power and divine nature, have been clearly perceived, ever since the creation of the world, in the things that have been made. So they are without excuse. *For although they knew God, they did not honor him as God or give thanks to him, but they became futile in their thinking, and their foolish hearts were darkened.* (Rom. 1:18–21)

Jesus Himself reaffirmed that our thoughts were of utmost importance when He shifted God's covenants with man from external demands to internal demands. The law gave way to grace. Sin was redefined as primarily a matter of the heart, and inner loyalty was the new standard.

The Sermon on the Mount, Christ's longest recorded sermon, is replete with references to this subtle but significant change in God's expectations for mankind. Jesus spoke about lust being equated with adultery. He said that unforgiveness was tantamount to condemning others. He said tithing only made sense when it was from a joyful heart. No longer was it enough to avoid murder; now hate was judged, and the new standard was love.

We can apply these truths and principles to more modern-day concerns as well. The main danger of drunkenness, for example, is that it alters our ability to think clearly. The jeopardy of an emotional affair is that it causes our brains to fuse connection with feelings that lead to dangerous patterns.

Our thoughts matter. Rarely do the blatant challenges to our thinking take us down, but the treacherously subtle shifts can. We're like the oblivious frog slowly being boiled in a pot of increasingly heated water.

It Always Goes Back to the Garden . . .

How did we get here? Why can't we just do the right thing? Why can't we hear truth one time and have it stick forever? Why do we have so little control over our minds?

I'm convinced that any sermon I've ever preached and any bit of advice I've ever given begins in the garden of Eden. Everything we see in humans today is rooted in the Tree of the Knowledge of Good and Evil.

Mankind is broken. God's image in us is tarnished. We are not good people struggling to continue our goodness; we are bad people at the core being rescued and redeemed by an all-loving God.

Adam and Eve were the best of us: unadulterated humanity, good, pure, and perfect. But the day they ate the fruit that God told them not to eat, all of that changed. With their rebellion, sin entered the world and chaos was unleashed. Moral entropy has haunted us ever since.

I don't blame them, to be honest; I would have done the same thing in their shoes. If our champions couldn't handle it, we certainly couldn't have handled it. But as humans learned the cost of disobedience to a holy and righteous God, we also undid the fabric of our spiritual reality. All that was beautiful in us became ugly.

Sin polluted our very cells and remapped our minds. As humanity left that garden, we lost our way and became very dangerous people.

When mankind says no to God, bad things happen.[3] And we say no to Him—a lot. When sin went viral in the world, it lodged itself in our cores.

God and His will are the epitome of Good and Right. Sin is a deviation, a distortion of how God designed things to be. Just as cancerous cells are renegade cells violating the purpose they were created for, so too are sinful minds and choices a violation of God's order of things. God intends the best for us; sin wrecks that.

. . . And Leads to the Cross

If you do not yet know the saving grace of the Lord Jesus Christ and the love He demonstrated on the cross by dying for your sins, now is the time to engage with that truth. It's silly to talk about accessing the power God has given us if we have not opened our souls to His presence. Our only shot in this endeavor is to partner with God for the cleanup once He has already done the impossible: rescued our souls.

I'll make this simple. God knows our plight. He knows we are hopelessly lost. When Adam and Eve threw away our birthright, He launched a redemption plan. That plan came to fruition approximately two thousand years ago, when God entered humanity and joined us where we were, in all our messiness. Doing all that we could not do, the God-Man, Jesus Christ, offered up His perfect life—not only to satisfy our debt of sin, but also to trade with us, the lost, so that we might be found and set free. When we receive that offer, we admit we are sinners, bad guys, broken at the core, resistant to God's will. Then we ask God to release the beautiful gift He has waiting for us—the forgiveness of our sins and the grace that wholly cleanses us. We then affirm that from here on out, we are His. We acknowledge that He is the King and His way is right. His plan of remaking us is now our plan. We offer open hearts in which He can dwell by the power of His Holy Spirit so that we are never alone—not now, not ever.

This is the solution—the *only* solution—to the core problem of sin, which we will never resolve ourselves. If you have not engaged with God in this manner, please take time to consider it now and begin your own relationship with Him today. Everything I have to say beyond this point is built upon this foundation, and it will neither make sense nor matter if this cornerstone is not set in your life.

Will it solve everything? Yes and no. It will solve all that truly matters (our sin nature). But will it make your life easy and problem free? Hardly.

Why Christians Still Struggle

Even we whom God has saved and redeemed—we who have admitted our real state and released our command centers over to Him to renew and remake—are still weighed down by sin. Salvation is the beginning of freedom, but releasing sinful habits, mind-sets, and identities takes a lifetime. That's why the Christian life is not as clean, polished, or easy as we'd like. Christ does the heavy lifting, but even the dusting is difficult.

Although the salvation offered on the cross allows us to be *born again*, restarted with a new nature, there is plenty left to do. We are still living with a broken rudder and a crooked keel. We drift no matter how hard we grip the wheel. But why do we fall short if the Lord has made us right? Because we still deal with the impact of sin. Our sin nature has been removed, but we still wrestle with patterns, identity, habits, influences, weakness, distortion, confusion, and the process of learning and maturing in our new nature. From the moment of conversion, the Holy Spirit works overtime to weed out whatever in us still stands contrary to God's will for our lives. It is that process that He invites us to join. And it is that process that this book is centered on. There is a way to transformation. It is a hard one, but we are not alone.

Sometimes we are tempted to give up under the weight of all that needs to be gotten rid of and renewed in our lives. I've felt this personally, and the apostle Paul knew this feeling as well. Romans 7 gives us a sneak peek into how he viewed his struggle.

> For *I do not understand my own actions. For I do not do what I want, but I do the very thing I hate.* . . . So now it is no longer I who do it, but sin that dwells within me. For I know that nothing good dwells in me, that is, in my flesh. *For I have the desire to do what is right, but not the ability to carry it out. For I do not do the good I want, but the evil I do not want is what I keep on doing.* . . . So I find it to be a law that when I want to do right, evil lies close at hand. For I delight in the law of God, in my inner being, but *I see in my members another law waging war against the law of my mind and making me captive to the law of sin that dwells in my members. Wretched man that I am! Who will deliver me from this body of death? Thanks be to God through Jesus Christ our Lord!* (vv. 15–25)

Rather than salvation causing us to be content with our situation, it only highlights the tension and intensifies our longing to be rid of the effects of sin. When the light bursts into our dark spirits, we realize for the first time that we are built for another place, another way. Eternity awakens in our hearts, and we begin to see a dream of what will be when someday we're the people God created us to be. This revelation only illuminates the remaining wickedness and brokenness within our hearts. This tension makes us long for home—heaven—where we know that all will be rectified and we will be at peace.[4] In the meantime, we ache to be set free along with the rest of creation, which already knows that things won't be fully right until the return of the King.[5]

The Blind Leading the Blind Through a Minefield

We are our own worst enemies. I believe the majority of the drama in our lives is self-caused. We are naturally self-destructive and prone to rebellion. But we have to deal not only with distortions within but also with attacks from the outside. In fact, at least three other major factors outside of our own complicated minds affect our lives on a daily basis.

The Bible says that we have three enemies: the flesh (our own madness), the world (systems contrary to God and perpetuated by broken people), and the Devil (a real and personal evil being, and his team with him). We'll talk about these in more detail in the next two chapters, but for now it's enough to say that we've got our work cut out for us. When Jesus looked at the mess mankind was in, He described us as "harassed and helpless, like sheep without a shepherd" (Matt. 9:36).

Where Is God? In the Other Garden

Perhaps the picture I'm painting is leaving you exasperated and screaming, "God, where are You? Why would You leave all of us little monsters running around hurting each other and only making things worse?" I feel your pain, and I understand your questions. Although I cannot answer everything about individual examples of suffering, I can tell you God's big-picture plan. I can share why I am so hopeful that, although we live as broken among other dangerous people, with an enemy hunting us down, God has a plan, and He is greater than all of our struggles.

Allow me to take you into yet another garden—this time the Garden of Gethsemane. Just as sin entered the world through the first garden (Eden), so was sin being prepped to be conquered in the second (Gethsemane) some eight to ten thousand years later. On the night that Jesus was going to be betrayed by a member of His team, arrested, and led to a brutal death on the cross, He went to a garden to pray. It was there that He had to face the greatest test that anyone could ever face: Would He remain true to the plan laid out for Him by Father God, even if it meant physical and spiritual death and judgment for the sins of the world? Being fully man and fully God, Jesus Christ was said to have been so stressed that He sweat "like great drops of blood" while He wept (Luke 22:44). It was in the garden that He chose to do the unthinkable so that we might be rescued. By the end of that prayer time, He was certain that He would fulfill the plan of God, fixing what was so deeply broken so that we might be protected and saved. The Sinless One agreed to die for sins that we committed, for a people who stood opposed to Him—the perfect for the imperfect.[6]

Transformation's Alpha and Omega

The Bible says that on the cross Jesus paid for our sins—all of them. He gave up His life with three words that changed both history and the future: "It is finished" (John 19:30). When God says something is finished, it's finished. The sin that stands against us is done away with. He fixed it once and for all.[7] He made us, in that moment, pure and holy, and He reconnected our relationship with God. The fancy term for all of that is *justification*. We were made right.[8] The Bible sums it up this way: "So if the Son sets you free, you will be free indeed" (John 8:36).

A Christian's entire identity needs to be shaped by this reality of what Christ did on the cross. It makes all the difference. We no longer live the same way as everyone else on the planet. We are new creations[9] and partakers of the divine nature.[10] The core of our identities has been changed out, but the process of renewal doesn't end there. The majority of our lives from now on is focused on learning what a new life means and how to live it out.

Hebrews 12:2 states that Jesus is not only the founder and author of our faith, but He is also the perfecter of our process of transformation. He is just as good at finishing as He is at beginning. Paul the apostle explained it this way:

> I am sure of this, that *he who began a good work in you will bring it to completion* at the day of Jesus Christ. (Phil. 1:6)

> Now may *the God of peace himself sanctify you completely,* and may your whole spirit and soul and body be kept blameless at the coming of our Lord Jesus Christ. *He who calls you is faithful; he will surely do it.* (1 Thess. 5:23–24)

I firmly believe that we live in a *Kingdom of Now but Not Yet.* That means that although Jesus Christ has begun a great work in us and in the world, it is not done yet. Although the most important work is finished, the mop-up job is still in process. This is why it seems that some things are complete and others are left undone. Understanding this concept helps us process how the Lord is on the throne but the world is not yet subject to Him. It explains why our nature is changed but our lives are still a work in progress.

God is on the job, and He knows what He's doing. From His vantage point, things should be far easier for us than they are. He completed the most important part, so the majority of what we need to do is let Him have His way and release all the trash that He wants to take out of our lives. Jesus talked about His preferred plan this way: "Come to me, all who labor and are heavy laden, and I will give you rest. Take my yoke upon you, and learn from me, for I am gentle and lowly in heart, and you will find rest for your souls. For *my yoke is easy, and my burden is light*" (Matt. 11:28–30).

Traditional religion tells us that it's all on us, that it's our job to be better on our own and to please God through more effort and sheer willpower. That's not only exhausting; it's impossible. Imagine living your life trying to weigh each moment to see if you've done enough good things to enter God's presence. Imagine trying to handle every situation perfectly so you aren't rejected by God. How would we ever get out from under the pile of shame and rejection?

Jesus introduced another way: the way of grace, where He cleans us up. As we talk in the following chapters about how we can improve our thinking, we'll keep this perspective in mind. It's not only about us and what we do. It's also about letting Him have His way in our lives.

The rest of this book will discern the nuances of what He wants for us and what needs to change in the way we think. How do we align with the identity He has given us? How do we change our minds (repent) and follow His direction (believe)? How do we fight the enemies of the flesh, the world, and the Devil? How do we deal with the monsters of compulsion, anger, anxiety, and depression? How do we train ourselves to remember that He is the King of our minds and hearts?

God's way is low-drama, peaceful, and right. Most of our current pain and frustration stem from our resistance to His way. The remnants of our old nature fight against what He wants, and that tension is exhausting. We still don't like what He likes or hate what He hates. Although He promises us difficulty in this world due to persecution, most of our struggles seem to come when we cling unnecessarily to sinful habits.

We fear losing things that we never should have held on to. We mourn the loss of items designed to be temporary. We cry over self-inflicted wounds. We stress over things that Jesus said don't matter. We doubt His goodness despite His consistent record. We willingly remain in the cages He already unlocked. We reshackle the chains He broke off.

Much of what we define as suffering comes from a distorted perspective. Sometimes, suffering is in the eye of the beholder, defined not by the action itself but the event surrounding it. Take, for example, the mind-set of a martyr. Scripture refers to men and women who chose not to be released but rather chose to die so that they might "obtain a better resurrection" (Heb. 11:35 NKJV). To them the relationship with God meant more than the suffering they endured.

Imagine if what we did in the gym (lifting heavy weights, completing extreme workouts, being pushed beyond exhaustion, having a heightened heart rate, and so on) was forced on us. We would consider that torture. But make it voluntary, and we do it willingly—and even pay for it—because we're looking toward weight loss or increased strength. If we know a valuable reason, we can go through anything. Without a heavenly perspective, this world seems random, hopeless, and cruel. But through the eyes of a believer, we find purpose, meaning, and an ultimate answer. So much of the needed renewal of our minds comes through a simple perspective shift.

Where Do We Begin?

Let's begin by not making it worse. Jesus cleans up and clears out our hearts, but we keep putting bad stuff back in. How about we stop the flow of devastation, and then we can talk about how to partner with God in the cleanup? The Holy Spirit can take out the trash fairly fast, but if we are bringing in stuff by the truckload, we are kidding ourselves if we expect significant transformation.

We have a crucial role in how we shape the terrain of our

minds. We can't get rid of all outside influences, but we can purposefully focus on filtering our inputs. We can stop the bleeding and build with purpose instead.

But there is still one more thing to do on the outset of our journey together: decide that we want change. We no longer want to be tossed on the winds of our own distorted thoughts. We want to have the Master's Mind—to align our thoughts and identities with God's.

Changing the way we think is difficult. It won't happen on its own. If we are to wade into our deep, dark psyches, then we need to be prepared to engage in warfare, or at least some significant repair. Ironically, an important factor in whether we will be able to bring our minds under control is a firm determination to see it through. The first step in changing our minds is a change of mind.

Chapter 2

Identity Theft

A recent fraud study reported that 15.4 million US consumers fell victim to identity theft in 2016, resulting in losses of $16 billion.[2] Identity theft occurs when someone steals another person's personal information and uses it for his or her own gain.

Perhaps one of the most unusual stories—for irony, if nothing else—is what happened to the former CEO of LifeLock, Todd Davis. LifeLock is a company that provides online protection from identity theft to more than three million subscribers.[2] Davis was so confident of his company's product that he became famous back in the early 2000s for including his real Social Security number in public advertising.

As of 2010, Todd Davis reportedly had been the victim of identity theft at least thirteen times.[3] We get the point: even the most assured can get hacked. What some would consider impenetrable simply is not. And just as virtual identity can be compromised, so too can emotional and spiritual identity.

We have been ripped off. Our identities—who we think we are—have been compromised, and we must reclaim them. As I mentioned earlier, the thieves are the flesh, the world, and the Devil. I will spend chapter 3 on the third thief, the Devil, so in this chapter let's take some time to investigate the first two hijackers, figure out what they have stolen or perverted, and learn how to make our identities stronger than they were before.

Why Are We Here?

Understanding the full impact of the theft in our souls is difficult if we don't first know who and whose we are. Our thoughts operate from our identities. Who we think we are affects the way we view the world and every situation we encounter. Reclaiming our true identities is critical to developing the Master's Mind. Let us begin then with a reminder of what we are and why we are here.

We are the property of God. We are His creations, and He made us for two primary reasons: for His glory and for relationship with Him. Whatever our lives are to be about, they must link back to God's intent at creation.

What does it mean to be created for someone's glory? Glory is what makes someone look good. We were designed to allow God to look good. Look good to whom? To the "great cloud of witnesses" that surrounds us (Heb. 12:1 NIV). It's not only the natural world—such as our neighbors, our families, and our friends—that watches what we do; it's also the supernatural world of heavenly and fallen beings. It's as if we are on a cosmic stage, and God is the director. All eyes are drawn to the work of the Creator.

Additionally, we were designed for relationship with God. God didn't create us because He was lonely or because He needed anything; God is completely self-satisfied. But God is so full of love and blessing that He desires to pour them out on His creation. It's similar to why so many of us choose to have children—not to fill a void in our souls but, rather, because we feel our hearts spill over with love and want to pour it out on someone who will be truly ours to care for, provide for, and protect.

Therefore, to accomplish these two primary goals, God created us in His image. The Bible says it this way:

> Then God said, "*Let us make man in our image, after our likeness.* And let them have dominion over the fish of the sea and over the birds of the heavens and over the livestock and over all the earth and over every creeping thing that creeps on the earth." *So God created man in his own image, in the image of God he created him; male and female he created them.* (Gen. 1:26–27)[4]

To be made in His image means that we are like Him; there are similarities between Him and us. God built into mankind some of His own incredible characteristics—creativity, reason, purpose, meaning, value, strength, dominion, vision, compassion, a relational nature, and the ability to love, to name a few. *Likeness* means "of the same type" and was more commonly used to refer to a man fathering a son.[5] Although we are not as exact a likeness as Jesus Christ, who is literally the "image of the invisible God" (Col. 1:15),[6] from birth we contain significant similarities to God, such as the ability to reason, to create, to love, to establish personal community, and so on. What is beautiful is that God's not done after we are born. His next step is to awaken in us another level of living, which He defines as a "new nature" or making us a "new creation" through spiritual rebirth in salvation (conversion). From there, He grows and directs us to look more and more like the perfect image His Son reflects.[7]

What Is God Like?

We need to know more about who God is and what He is like if we are to do serious work on our identities. We cannot form a vision until we know the goal, and we cannot assess progress until we know the standard. We can always read the Word of God to learn more about Him, and classics such as A. W. Tozer's *The Knowledge of the Holy* or J. I. Packer's *Knowing God* offer opportunities for deeper study and exploration.

Yet it's not only knowing *about* God that's important; it's knowing Him personally. The more we know Him, the more we are transformed and the more aligned our minds become with His. As long as our knowledge remains principle only, we are unchanged. If there is no emotional connection, no depth of relationship, no alteration of our way of life, then connection has not taken root.

Who we believe ourselves to be directly correlates with what we believe about where we come from, who made us, and what our purpose is. Therefore, a healthy grasp of God and His nature will lay an immovable foundation upon which we can build an understanding of our true identities. So, what is God like?

- He is loving and kind.[8]
- He is all-powerful and in control (sovereign).[9]
- He is all-knowing (omniscient).[10]
- He is everywhere at once (omnipresent).[11]
- He is the Creator and Sustainer of the world.[12]
- He is merciful and gracious.[13]
- He is relational and personable.[14]
- He is joyful and satisfied.[15]
- He is just, right, and good.[16]
- He is loyal and trustworthy.[17]
- He is compassionate and empathetic.[18]
- He is full of creativity and imagination.[19]
- He is absolutely healthy and whole, lacking nothing.[20]

How many of these attributes do we long for, only to be discouraged by our limitations, hang-ups, and sin? Don't these make a checklist of what we hope to be transformed into? Sure, we don't expect to be omniscient, omnipresent, or sovereign, but don't we know deep down that God built us for more? Don't we sense that the ways our minds work are not aligned with His?

We were patterned after the nature of God. God wants to build these qualities within us, to shape us into people more like Him. The Master's plan for us is to have the Master's Mind.

A More Tangible Example

Trying to follow the role model of an invisible God is hard. Perhaps it's easier to consider Jesus, who is a perfect example of how God's image looks in humanity. In fact, I would suggest that one of the primary reasons the Second Person of the Trinity became human was to provide us an example to work from and a goal for us to mature into. As I stated before, Jesus is the "image of the invisible God." The author of Hebrews described it this way:

> Long ago, at many times and in many ways, God spoke to our fathers by the prophets, but in these last days *he has spoken to us by his Son*, whom he appointed the heir of all things, through whom also he created the world. *He is the radiance of the glory of God and the exact imprint of his nature.* (Heb. 1:1–3)

If Jesus is the "exact imprint" of God's nature, then He is the perfect example for us to follow because He lived, like us, in this broken world. He had to demonstrate what a life submitted to the Master's will looks like. He struggled and was tempted. He had needs and losses. He experienced fear, anxiety, and sadness. Yet His identity remained grounded in His Father, and His mind was firmly fixed on His true nature as the Son of God.

Therefore, if we want to find out what it looks like to be compassionate, we look at Christ healing a leper through touch. If we want to find an example of patience in stressful circumstances, we look at His response to the constant attacks from religious leaders and His obedience under intense pressure in the Garden of Gethsemane. If we want to model our mind-sets after someone fully surrendered to the plans of God, we look at the pathway to the cross. Jesus operated from His identity as the Son of God, which was confirmed verbally by the Father at His baptism, by John the Baptist,[21] and again at the Mount of Transfiguration.[22] His thoughts were laser focused on the Father's will at all times. He was immovable in His determination and purpose. Regardless of the influence of the flesh, the world, or the Devil, Jesus' mind was secure and ordered.

So Who Are We?

You and I are not Jesus, but because of what He accomplished on the cross, we are far more like Him than most of us imagine. It's true that He was born sinless (pure humanity like Adam and Eve), and we were born into sin (original sin that entered the world after the fall). It's true that each time we have sinned in the past we have dug a hole for ourselves that He never had to claw out of. It's true that we struggle with habit patterns that Jesus never allowed to take hold in His own life. It's true that His connection to the Father—the conduit by which their communication was shared—was clean, pure, and holy. So, yes, Jesus was working with a different deck of cards. However, His rescue gave us a fighting chance to follow His example and live the way He lived. Although we are soiled by sin and born with a sinful nature, the significance of our rebirth into a new creation cannot be overstated.

The Bible says the following things are true for Christians because Jesus died for our sins:

- **We have a new nature in Christ.** We are new creations. The old is gone, and all things have become new. We can start fresh and live a life pleasing to God.[23]
- **We are loved and cherished by God,** not because we have done anything to deserve that love, but because He is filled with love and pours it out on us. Even our failure cannot diminish His love. He initiated our relationship, not us.[24]
- **We are children of God** with all the benefits, resources, authority, and power that come with that position.[25] Therefore we are part of the family of God, joined together with all true believers throughout time.[26]
- **We are made right in the eyes of God**—holy, justified, forgiven, and cleansed.[27]
- **We are free from condemnation** for our sin. When God the Father sees us, He sees righteousness.[28]
- **We no longer have to sin.** We have a choice to do things God's way. We are not forced to sin, nor are we ignorant of our choices to sin. We are empowered to do what is right.[29]
- **We are certain of a secure and glorious future.** Jesus awaits us in a heaven prepared perfectly for us.[30]
- **We are effective.** As we remain connected to God, He allows us to partner with Him to bring transformation to the world around us. We are assured that what He calls us and empowers us to do *will* bear much fruit.[31]
- **We are indwelt by God** through His Son and Holy Spirit so that we are never alone, abandoned, or powerless.[32]

The First Hijacker: The Flesh

When the heart of mankind turned from God, the perfect, unhindered relationship with Him was lost. Humanity began to be hostile in mind toward God,[33] and our sinful nature took hold, warring against all that God wants for us. Thankfully, Jesus Christ came to repair and restore the broken system, but tremendous ramifications still reverberate in our universe.

The *flesh* is a term the Bible uses to describe unregenerate humanity. That's a fancy way of identifying the aspects of us that aren't aligned with God—the stuff that's not fixed yet. It's the tension we feel when we know what we ought to do but can't seem to get it done. Sometimes it's the sneaky, tempting feeling to put our hands in the cookie jar, and sometimes it's the prison that won't let us out. The flesh is responsible for the majority of the internal battles we face.

The flesh is selfish at the core. Its remaining habit patterns keep us going back to garbage when God has better bread for us. It's the Gollum in us that obsesses over things and refuses to let go despite the consequences. It's what leads us down the pathways that God told us not to tread. It tells us we're out for personal gratification, that we live for the moment and aren't made for more. It makes us think we're enslaved by our passions and desires.

Let's be clear: the metaphorical flesh is not our literal flesh, our bodies. Those are neutral, not evil. The flesh is the mind-set, the distortion of identity, the internal dysfunction that keeps us doing the wrong things. It's the part of us that stands opposed to God and His will, the stuff we are trying to get out of our heads. Our bodies can be brought into submission; the flesh must be removed.

Our flesh doesn't want to go, and it's not going to go quietly. Paul talked about it extensively in the book of Romans. After sharing his personal struggles, he set forward a plan to help Christians deal with it:

There is therefore now no condemnation for those who are in Christ Jesus. For the law of the Spirit of life has set you free in Christ Jesus from the law of sin and death. For God has done what the law, weakened by the flesh, could not do. *By sending his own Son* in the likeness of sinful flesh and for sin, *he condemned sin in the flesh*, in order that the righteous requirement of the law might be fulfilled *in us, who walk not according to the flesh but according to the Spirit. For those who live according to the flesh set their minds on the things of the flesh, but those who live according to the Spirit set their minds on the things of the Spirit. For to set the mind on the flesh is death, but to set the mind on the Spirit is life and peace.* (Rom. 8:1–6)

The plan is rather simple: Jesus sets us free from the flesh and allows us to walk in the Spirit. It's our job to set our minds on the Spirit and receive the life and peace God has promised us. In other words, Jesus breaks the chains, and we learn what it is to live out our new identities as free people and children of God. The challenge is unlearning what has been built in us from birth.

Consider the struggle of a young woman who was adopted into a new family as a teenager. She has already experienced a family (or families). She has already developed thoughts and patterns influenced by her circumstances. She already has habits and a relatively developed worldview. But now she finds herself in a new home with a new family, a new set of rules, new resources, new dynamics, and a whole new opportunity at life. Although it's wonderful, it's also scary and complicated. Little by little she trusts and tests the love and boundaries around her to see what will hold. With each passing year, she settles into her new identity.

The same is true of us when we first accept Christ's sacrifice and become children of God. At first this new identity seems too good to be true, and we are suspicious. When we finally believe that God has made such a wonderful offer, we reject it, because if God only knew what we've done, He wouldn't offer it at all. Then when we finally accept His offer, it doesn't fit. We try on the clothes, but they are too big, or they feel funny. Like breaking in new sneakers, developing a new identity in Christ takes a while. It may need a lot of use and engagement before it feels comfortable.

With a new identity, family, and life come new expectations and responsibilities. The new home contains a new culture. Suddenly we are aware of freedoms that have never been available and healthy boundaries that weren't there before. Chores show up on our to-do list, and caring correction reveals itself. All of this seems like too much at first. What we need to remember is that our Father would never expect the things He does if He hadn't first given us the ability to do them. God's calling is God's enabling; never forget that. If God asks or commands us to do something, that is a guarantee that He has already provided the means for us to do it.

The Second Hijacker: The World

The Bible says that in addition to wrestling with our flesh, we also have the enemy of *the world*. What does that mean?

The Greek word for *world* used in the New Testament is *kosmos*. It's a complex word that means everything from the physical planet Earth to human life to godless systems. The definition for each use must therefore be found in context. The type of *kosmos* I am interested in is the one that represents what stands against God: the systems, beliefs, and ideologies in the culture around us that are contrary to God and His truth. It's the non-God part of our society.[34] Under this definition, the world is strongly opposed to God ruling it and bringing it under control. It's the logical outcome when you have a personal evil being who lures humanity to reject God and His ways. It creates a whole race of rebellion, and that's exactly what we are facing. When rebellious hearts set up systems of living that aren't God-honoring, you get the world we have today, with all of its selfish, humanistic, and antagonistic views, expressions, and opinions. We see this view most blatantly in anti-God messages made popular by Nietzsche's assertion that "God is dead," atheistic propaganda, unapologetic debauchery, and the like. More subtly, you will find it packaged in any product based in selfishness, which permeates most of our advertising.

This world is what makes Christians feel out of place—as though we don't belong here.[35] The Bible speaks of the world as the part of our universe and existence that Satan rules and runs.[36] Although we live here on a fallen planet, among people of this world, we are called by God neither to follow those influences nor to let them mold our minds, guide our decisions, or shape our identities.[37]

But how do we escape or resist its impact? It's all around us—and therein lies the problem. The vast majority of influences around us point to things other than God. What our society values is not what God values. What they love He may hate. The priority lists are different, and so are the agendas and goals. It's as if the world is the polar opposite of God's ways. This is why the apostle John was so severe in his teachings on the world:

> Do not love the world or the things in the world. If anyone loves the world, the love of the Father is not in him. For all that is in the world—the desires of the flesh and the desires of the eyes and pride of life—is not from the Father but is from the world. And the world is passing away along with its desires, but whoever does the will of God abides forever. (1 John 2:15–17)

John was only taking a page from His best friend, Master, and King, Jesus, who said, "For what does it profit a man to gain the whole world and forfeit his soul?" (Mark 8:36).

It is the world that tells us we are number one, the center of the universe, when in fact God is. It's the world that tells us to give way to all of our passions and to indulge in anything that feels good because pleasure is an end in itself. It's the world that tells us we should scratch and claw to get more stuff we don't need so that we feel superior to those around us. It's the world that tells us we are accidents, mere random chance resulting from primordial ooze. It's the world that tells us we will never have enough until we get a little bit more. It's the world that suggests that unless we get the approval—no, the applause or worship—from others, we have no significance. It's the world that teaches us about the almighty dollar. It's the world that tells us this life is all we get, so we'd better live it up and burn our bridges along the way.

The world drives us toward the Facebook life. You know what I mean, right? A life that is all about appearances. We show (post) only the best of us, and we hide behind the mask of pretend. As we sit alone in our rooms, we churn out image after image of active and fulfilling lives that are actually spent alone behind a camera. We live in anonymity, hiding behind a screen so we can promote fake lives while pretending there will be no consequences. Yet all the while our spirits call us back to the truth: life is not about self-exaltation but about exaltation of Christ alone.

We Are Not Alone

With all the negative influences and dysfunction in our lives—from the world around us to the flesh within us—no wonder our minds are out of control. It's time to get angry enough to do something about it. It's time to be purposeful about forming our own identities and not letting others shape them for us. Who is worthy to build our souls? Who gets to invest in our identities? Who's safe and wise enough to tell us what to think and help us master our minds? There is only One.

God.

Our responsibility is to partner with God in the development of our identities. He gives us the plans; we implement them. He gives us the power; we use it rightly. He identifies the enemies; we avoid them or battle them.

What's so wonderful about knowing that we have supernatural help is that we can enjoy the process of transformation. Each struggle can be viewed as an opportunity to watch God move. Instead of fretting and hoping for a good outcome, we can engage, knowing that if God wants something, He will provide the way and means for us to have it. We may not understand that way and means, and He certainly won't reveal all the details of His plans, but if we are willing to trust that He cares even more about our healthy renovation and development than we do, our hearts can be at peace as we transform.

It's equally encouraging to remember that when Jesus gets done with us, we will look more like Him. Ultimately we'll be escorted into a glorious new world we have been perfectly designed for, where we can thrive. Today it's hard work; tomorrow it will be wonderful. When Jesus saved us, He called in the Holy Spirit to live in our hearts as a guarantee that, no matter what, we will be with Him where He is, and our futures are secure. Once the Lord is on the job, we get to watch the Master at work, unfolding the "eternity design" that was built into us in our mothers' wombs and warehoused in our souls. Because of this great hope and joy, we have the strength, vision, and power to reestablish the Master's Mind within us.

What Happens If We Don't Get Our Identities Back?

Perhaps the saddest and most tragic cost of not having a firm God-based identity is that we live in a way that's less than what God created us to be. If we were to see how God views us and what He intends for us, we would break down and sob. We have lived with so much less. We have compromised beauty for dirt. His glory has been diminished, and our sheen has worn off.

One of the incredible gifts God has given me as a pastor and shepherd of people is to see their potential. What I can see is only a tiny snippet of what God can see in us. He understands what He built. He knows what He designed. The truth of our future and hope is on the tip of His tongue. Even our sin can't stop His eyes from envisioning His children as holy, healthy, and free.

It's not that God is mad at us all the time for being failures. He knows the struggles we're facing far better than we do. It's that God wants the best for His children. Yes, God is mad, but He's angry at the bad guys, the enemies of His kids: the flesh, the world, and the Devil. And it's not that God doesn't understand the *process*—after all, He set the sanctification process in place. We are not supposed to be full, complete, or perfect yet. It's okay to be broken. It's okay to be a work in progress. But what He longs for is for us to be healthy and whole. Parents desperately love their children, and they want more for them or mourn when those children settle for less.

What Happens If We Do Get Them Back?

The benefits of a secure, God-based identity are incredible. Let's take a moment to dream of what it would look like if we truly let God order our minds and help us bring them under control. What are the rewards of knowing fully who we are? What would happen if we were secure and understood our true value? What would a self-controlled mind produce?

Jesus lived the life He was born to live because He knew who He was and why He was here. Every move He made came from His identity and purpose.

Christ accomplished everything He came to do by following one premise: obedience. He followed everything His Father told Him. He lived the life laid out for Him. He didn't spend time trying to come up with new ideas or new ways, and He certainly didn't waste time trying to be someone He wasn't. But how was He able to be obedient in all things? Why wasn't He hijacked like we are? Because He knew who He was and remained firmly grounded in that identity.

Jesus opened a significant conversation with His disciples with an important question: "Who do people say that I am?" It was a question about public perception of His identity. The disciples threw out a few names of respected prophets and miracle workers, and Jesus let those sit in the air for a moment. And then He asked the more crucial question: "But who do you say that I am?" It's one thing to know what the masses say, but what the disciples thought about Him would determine their relationship to Him personally. Peter blurted out, "You are the Christ, the Son of the living God."[38]

Jesus affirmed that Peter was right. He also explained that the only reason Peter knew the correct answer was because the Father in heaven was revealing who Christ really was. In essence, Jesus allowed His disciples to consider all opinions. He then zeroed in on who He really was, and from that platform He made some incredible statements. He told them that because of who He knew Himself to be, He had to live a life directed toward the cross, a pathway full of persecution. He also told them that who He was had a direct impact on who *they* were and what they would do. The disciples were the beginning of a new movement He was establishing on earth—a church, an extension of His ministry, His body. He told them that through that extension He would transform the world, and the Enemy would not be able to shut it down. In other words, who He was transformed who the disciples were and made them into world changers. This is the same transformation Jesus offers to you and me.

Grasping Grace

Any discussion on making significant changes in our lives, even with the Lord's help and power, must include the concept of grace. If it doesn't, we will find ourselves creating a performance religion and ruining the point of our adoption as children of God. Perhaps no other concept of our relationship with Jesus Christ is so significant yet so rarely fully grasped. Because grace violates our normal way of doing things, God's extension of grace to us seems not just improbable but impossible. Nevertheless, it's true.

Author and disciple-maker Kenneth Boa said in his book *Conformed to His Image*, "Grace teaches us that the most important thing about us is not what we do, but who and whose we are in Christ. In Scripture, doing (our actions) should flow out of being (our identity); the better we grasp our identity in Christ, the more our actions should reflect Christlike character."[39]

Maybe you need to read it again to let it sink in: "The most important thing about us is not what we do, but who and whose we are in Christ." How powerful is that?

Please don't hear in my words a performance-driven theology. We do not deserve God's love or His salvation, yet He has extended it to us. He started the relationship, not us, and the success or failure of that bond rests squarely on Him alone. If left to us, we will ruin it all. He knows that. All He asks is that we stop fighting and let Him do what He does best—be our Savior and King. Paul the apostle wrote, "Therefore, since we have been justified by faith, *we have peace with God* through our Lord Jesus Christ. Through him we have also obtained access by faith *into this grace in which we stand, and we rejoice* in hope of the glory of God" (Rom. 5:1–2).

By definition, grace is "undeserved favor." Grace isn't earned; rather, it's given out of the goodness of someone else's heart. But hearing the definition and believing it for our lives are two different things. Practically, for a Christian, grace means that when Jesus said He was finished with our problem of sin, it was finished. We are no longer defined by our sin, and it's not the most important thing about us. Grace means that when God says He loves us, He's not lying or tricking us. It means He not only loves us but likes us. It means He is not going away. It means there is nothing we can do to make God love us any more or any less than He does right now.

When grace settles into our minds and identities, things around us start to make sense. Suddenly our relationships no longer need to be based on affirmation for a desperate heart. We no longer do things to earn favor with God, but we rest in what He's already done. Our motives are purified, and we stop scrambling for meaning and value.

Grace even cuts at the heart of the oldest and greatest of sins: pride. The same sin that caused the fall of Lucifer stirs in our souls. It's easy to slip into pride when we see how God has built us and valued us. Made in His image, we are beautiful and extraordinary, the pinnacle of His creation. It is there, in those thoughts, that we begin to lose our way, believing that we deserve the applause and credit. But grace teaches us that everything we have is a gift. We adjust back into the mind-set of undeserved favor and shake off the haze of pride. We're restored to the understanding that we are built and sustained entirely by God. Once grace takes hold again, we experience peace.

The Freedom a Fully Formed Identity Brings

It's difficult to obey God when we are worried about affirmation from others. It's hard to be pure when our cravings are out of control. It's almost impossible to be consistent when our minds are all over the place. But when we know who we are, when we know our value, when we are secure in our purpose, when we harness our minds in alignment with God's, we are freed from our defensive postures, and we go on the offensive. Not only are we healthy, but we also become a significant threat to the kingdom of darkness that does most of its work through bullying the insecure.

If we know who we are, we live intentionally, purposefully. We are able to regulate our emotions and respond to others in a healthy way instead of lashing out from defensiveness. We are able to bridle our spirits and be driven by God's direction rather than by ambition and competitiveness. Our passions are brought under control to do what they were designed to do: bring flavor into life.

When we know who God is and who we are in light of Him, our relationship with Him deepens, and we connect with Him not as a servant but as a son or daughter. When we know His thoughts about us, we are free from fear of rejection. When we understand grace, we are no longer driven to perform for others' acceptance. We shift away from mere sin management to a deeper, more authentic Christian existence. We begin to do things because they are right and not out of fear.

Our relationships take on a completely different tone. We are able to love because we are filled up with love and have an abundance to share. We are joyful because we realize all that matters has been secured already by Jesus Christ, and our futures are certain and beautiful. We are peaceful because our capable and loving Father is looking out for our best interests. We have patience because we are no longer fighting for significance. We are kind to others because we are not in competition with them. We are good, not because we try harder but because we are simply living out our new nature. We are faithful to our commitments because we know others are relying on us and we choose to be men and women of our word. We are gentle because God has been gentle with us and not harsh. And we live with self-control because we take advantage of all the freedoms and power the Holy Spirit provides us by living inside us. We are not perfect, but we are healthy.

Peaceful with Process

As we conclude this chapter and consider the work we need to do on our identities, let me reiterate that it's okay to be in process. The goals I put forth in this book are just that—goals. I don't expect anyone to be perfect or even significantly different overnight. I want to cast a vision of what could be (and, to be honest, what should be). I never want you to hear me speaking down to you (since I'm in process too!) or feel judged for being a work in progress. God designed us to grow incrementally. He knows how long it takes to change a life. He knows the complications and the challenges. And He's okay with it. He's far more concerned with the direction we are headed than how far we've gone down the road.

We need to realize that loving God doesn't automatically make us healthy. Being saved doesn't make us mature. Desperately wanting things to be different now doesn't mean they will be different right away. That's not how it works. It's hard to be patient and let God have His way, especially when He seems to work at a snail's pace. But how much of that is due to our resistance, and how much is due to the fact that He transforms things at the core for lasting change, not just temporary alteration? That takes time, and He's not in a rush.

God is infinitely more patient and understanding than we realize. He's not afraid of what's going to happen; He's in charge of it. He's not wondering how it's going to work out; He already knows. He's not wringing His hands over our lack of advancement;

He's putting another plan in place or simply waiting for the first to take effect.

If He has our hearts, He knows what to do with the rest. Be patient and trust Him. His ways always work.

Chapter 3

The Father of Lies

In chapter 2 we looked at two enemies of our souls and some of the ways they keep us from living our true identities in Christ and aligning with the Master's Mind—God's way of thinking about ourselves and our lives. God is working in us, and we can have faith in that process. But we also need to be aware of the biggest enemy of them all: the Devil.

The Devil is real, and he's a bad guy. He introduced the sin that brought down our world, he's a bully who picks on us every day, and he doesn't fight fair. He's the reason for a significant amount of the distortion of our identities and the chaos in our minds. So many people dismiss him as a figment of religious imagination or at least as a being far removed from their lives, but nothing could be further from the truth.

Listen to the apostle Peter: "Be sober-minded; be watchful. *Your adversary the devil prowls around like a roaring lion, seeking someone to devour. Resist him*, firm in your faith" (1 Peter 5:8–9).

Jesus told a parable that exposed the Devil's plan to distort and infiltrate our world and influence our identities and thoughts:

He put another parable before them, saying, "The kingdom of heaven may be compared to a man who sowed good seed in his field, but while his men were sleeping, *his enemy came and sowed weeds among the wheat* and went away. So when the plants came up and bore grain, then the weeds appeared also. And the servants of the master of the house came and said to him, '*Master, did you not sow good seed in your field? How then does it have weeds?*' He said to them, '*An enemy has done this.*' So the servants said to him, 'Then do you want us to go and gather them?' But he said, 'No, lest in gathering the weeds you root up the wheat along with them. Let both grow together until the harvest, and at harvest time I will tell the reapers, "Gather the weeds first and bind them in bundles to be burned, but gather the wheat into my barn."'" (Matt. 13:24–30)

Welcome to our lives. We didn't mean to plant bad stuff. We didn't knowingly stuff our minds with garbage. Our parents didn't mean to distort our identities. Our friends aren't trying to wreck us. The advertising agencies don't want to hurt us as much as they simply want our money. But if everyone is well-intentioned, how did things go so far south?

There's a personal evil running the show. There is an insidious plan to wreck what God loves—and that's us. There's a supernatural drama that is infinitely beyond us, but we are caught in the crossfire. When God chose to create us with His loving hands and place us on this earth, it was game on. We look like God and smell like God, and those of us who have given our lives over to Him are indwelt by God; we live for Him and glorify Him. We represent everything that Satan hates. Our very existences irritate him. Since he cannot kill us—God won't let him—his next move is to put us out of commission. Therefore, he will do anything in his power to distract, distort, shut down, destabilize, pollute, block, and minimize us. In his view, a disabled Christian is almost as good as a dead one.

It's difficult to sort out what parts of our identities are healthy and what's dysfunctional, because everything looks similar. That's the sneakiness of Satan's work. He's brilliant. He knows that what we believe and what we think shape our lives, so of course he will attack there first and foremost. However, he also knows we will resist anything that looks blatantly dangerous, so he wraps most of his distortions in familiar, tempting, and seemingly innocuous packaging. He retains his scary threats for his bullying work.

When you know the goal and the strategy of an enemy, you can defend and counterstrike appropriately. The purpose of this discussion is to expose the Devil's plans and methods and to prepare our minds for every attack.[1] In order to do that, we need a cursory understanding of who he is and what he wants.

Where He Came From

We don't know much about Satan's origin, his development, or his heart and mind. The Bible doesn't talk about him with a lot of specificity.[2] Although I have spent decades studying and teaching on this subject, the fact remains that solid information is spotty, and we are all trying to put together a puzzle from a pile of pieces that can fit in multiple ways.

We know Satan is a bad guy, but there's a good reason to think that at one time he was a good guy.[3] I am of the school that believes in Lucifer's fall from heaven—that Lucifer, once a cherubim of God,[4] His highest and most beautiful creation at the time,[5] caved to his pride and ambition[6] and waged a war to take God's throne. He ultimately lost the war and was cast out of heaven with the fallen angels who followed him.[7]

There in the darkness of Satan's new abode here on earth, God did a mighty work. He began to re-create, to reshape, to design a new world with light and beauty and glory. It was there—in a world dominated by angry celestial beings led by a leader consumed with hubris—that God made a man in His image to demonstrate to the heavenly world what it looks like when far lesser beings[8] love and follow a God they barely know,[9] unlike those angels who rebelled against God with relatively full knowledge.[10]

This new chapter had a challenging opening scene. It was not long before the beautiful, pure, and sinless new creation met a serpent with brand-new ideas.

What He's Like

By the time we meet Satan on earth, he is already consumed with hate,[11] an opponent of God, a master of deception, and the enemy of mankind.[12] A simple review of the names used for him in the Bible tells us a lot. The Hebrew word *Satan* means "accuser" or "opponent," implying that he is an enemy of both God and man. He is linked to the serpent that tempted Eve.[13] He is pictured as an accusing prosecutor in the story of Job and in a vision recorded in the book of Zechariah.[14] Even the name *Devil* (the Greek version of the Hebrew *Satan*) means "Accuser."[15] He is known as leader of demons,[16] prince of the power of the air and ruler of this world,[17] especially those that aren't Christians.[18] He is connected to images such as a dragon,[19] a hunting lion,[20] the Apollyon/destroyer,[21] the king of death,[22] the ruler of darkness,[23] and Leviathan.[24] But perhaps the most encompassing title for him is Evil One.[25]

Reading all the stories about him and gathering all the information we're given, we learn the following:

On One Hand

- **Satan is an evil genius.** He's brilliant and creative, far more intelligent than any human being. He not only possesses superior knowledge but also has the benefit of having watched mankind from the beginning; he understands humans' patterns and nature. He knows pretty much everything about us.

  As a pastor, I'm asked often whether Satan can read our thoughts. Maybe he can or maybe he can't, but it doesn't matter. With his extensive knowledge, he doesn't need to read our thoughts to know what we are thinking. He already knows. The bottom line is that we won't outsmart him.[26]

- **Satan is bigger, stronger, and faster than we are.** Satan was designed as a superior heavenly being. It is possible that he was the biggest and *baddest* angel of them all. Even a cursory glance at the Bible shows you the extraordinary power he wields. One angel can slaughter thousands of men. People who are merely possessed by a demon have superhuman strength. Satan is not limited by our time and space issues, so he can be anywhere he wants at any time, albeit in only one location at a time. (He's not omnipresent.) We will never win a battle of strength on our own.[27]

- **Satan can do significant damage.** Although he can't do everything, including anything God limits him from, Satan can create an awful lot of destruction. The Bible references demonic influence behind world events and natural disasters, and Satan's team can wreak havoc on the human body as well. They can cause physical illness,[28] insanity,[29] muteness,[30] deafness,[31] epilepsy,[32] blindness,[33] suicidal mania,[34] injury,[35] and defects.[36] They can torture the unsaved[37] and trouble our spirits, as they did to Saul.[38] We will not be able to defend ourselves from his attacks in our own power.

- **Satan is more organized than we are.** He has the ability to lead whole nations astray, whole people groups into lies, and whole cultures into embracing wickedness. We will not out-strategize him.[39]

- **We must not underestimate him, and he deserves our healthy respect.** There are a few places in Scripture where people are rebuked for not taking demonic power seriously, so let's not make that mistake. It's wise to respect enemies stronger than us and see them for what they are.[40]

On the Other Hand

- **Satan is created and limited.** Satan is not an equal and opposite superpower to God; the Bible does not teach duality. God is Creator, and Satan and demons are created. God is eternal; there was a time when demons didn't exist. They do not get to do whatever they want but are forced to submit to God's every command.[41]

- **Our Bodyguard is bigger, stronger, faster, and smarter than Satan.** As Christians, we are God's property. To mess with us is to mess with Him. We bear the seal and guarantee of the indwelling Holy Spirit, and Satan knows it. He can growl all he wants, but if he harms us, he answers to our King. When we read stories in the Gospels of Jesus casting out demons, we see their respect and fear of Him. They know who He is and are scared out of their minds of Him.[42] He has already shut down and cast out some demons into the abyss, which serves as a warning that at any moment He can do the same to the ones who remain.[43]

- **His hold on the world has been broken, and he's losing ground.**
  Once king of this world, Satan was decisively beaten by Jesus
  Christ when He came to earth. Christ's arrival meant that
  Satan's hold on the world was being challenged and diminished.[44] Instead of setting up His full kingdom and wiping
  out the Enemy just yet, Jesus began pressing in through His
  power and the power present in His saved people. Satan
  was judged again,[45] and he was bound and beaten down
  significantly through the ministry of Jesus,[46] with the most
  significant impact happening through the cross.[47] Yet let's
  be clear: although Satan's hold is broken and his kingdom
  constantly experiences defeat all over the world through the
  expanding kingdom of Christ, he's still alive and fighting.[48]
  Until Jesus returns to shut it all down, we live in complicated
  circumstances in which Satan continues to have a tight
  grasp on the world (primarily the nonbelieving world) even
  as Christ is breaking in.
- **Satan's end is sure.** He will be defeated once and for all, judged
  again (this time by us at Jesus' side[49]), and cast into the lake
  of fire to dwell there in torment forever. There is no question; his end is certain.[50]

What He Wants

Satan is angry and wants to hurt what God loves the most—
mankind, especially those who are born again as His children.[51]
Satan cannot directly attack God anymore; that ship has sailed,
and everyone remembers how it turned out. Heaven is locked, but
earth is still in play. So now Satan must attack the heart of God[52]
and attempt to thwart His plans here on earth.[53] His goal is to do
his best to alienate people from God.[54]

For those God calls His sons and daughters, there is remarkable limitation on what Satan can do to us. But if his way were unhindered,[55] he would destroy us. The New Testament tells us a story of a man who was under Satan's full control. There are three gospel accounts, which I will combine together to paraphrase the full story:

> **Then they sailed to the country of the Gerasenes/**<u>Gadarenes,</u> **which is opposite Galilee. When Jesus had stepped out** *of the boat,* **onto land,** *immediately* <u>two demon-possessed men met him, coming out of the tombs, so fierce that no one could pass that way.</u> **One of the men** *with an unclean spirit* **was from the city, but for a long time he had worn no clothes, and he had not lived in a house but among the tombs.** *No one could bind him anymore, not even with a chain, for he had often been bound with shackles and chains, but he wrenched the chains apart and broke the shackles in pieces. No one had the strength to subdue him. Night and day among the tombs and on the mountains he was always crying out and cutting himself with stones.* **When he saw Jesus** *from afar, he ran,* **cried out,** *and fell down before him. And* <u>behold, they cried out</u> *with a loud voice,* **"What have you to do with** <u>us,</u> **Jesus,** <u>O</u> **Son of the Most High God?** <u>Have you come here to torment us before the time?</u> **I beg you,** *I adjure you by God,* **do not torment me."** *For he was saying to him, "Come out of the man, you unclean spirit!"* **Jesus then asked him, "What is your name?" And he said,** *"My name is* **Legion,** *for we are many,"* **for many demons had entered him. And they begged him** *earnestly not to send them out of the country,* **not to command them to depart into the abyss.**[*]

---

[*] The paraphrase is composed from the following accounts: Matt. 8:28–34 (underlined text); Mark 5:1–20 (bold italic text); Luke 8:26–39 (bold text).

That, my friend, is Satan's will for our lives. If he had his way, we would all be tormented on the inside and destroyed on the outside. We would be fully under his control so that he could separate us from God and nullify our impact in this world for God's kingdom. He would distort our thoughts, steal our identities, and render us unrecognizable. Although God rarely lets Satan have his full way with either believers or unbelievers, even a partial fulfillment of Satan's plan for our lives is devastating. That is why our study is so important. We simply cannot allow Satan to have our minds, hearts, or souls. We cannot be ignorant of his schemes. We must know how he works so that we are able to stand our ground and fight back.

That Bible story is one of my favorites because of how it ends. That man who appears to be beyond hope, fully under the control of the Enemy, is set free by Jesus Christ. By the end of the story, he is dressed, in his right mind, and sitting at the feet of Jesus, a new man. Our God is so wonderful and so powerful! Praise His name!

As we go through the rest of this chapter, we should keep this image in mind. When we feel discouraged or nervous about what Satan can do to us, we need to remember that Jesus is far more powerful. It's important to know what Satan's up to and where he's trying to trip us up. But we do that not out of fear but out of wisdom. We want to know how much influence Satan has over us and how many traps we have fallen into. Where on the scale of Satan's will for our lives are we today? How much territory of our minds has he affected? That's worth talking about.

This Present Evil: His Strategies

Satan has hundreds of methods by which he seeks to steal our identities, diminish our effectiveness, and rob us of our joy.[56] I will mention just a few and then focus on the big one: deception.

- **Bullying through fear.** Satan is a bully who wants to scare us into submission. The power of fear is extraordinary. We will do incredible things to avoid death and will give up almost anything to remain safe. The Devil excels at using fear as a weapon. He knows what to say to freak us out and get us to back down. Fortunately for the believer, Jesus Christ shut down the fear of death with His miraculous rescue on the cross. Satan should have a much harder time scaring off Christians.
- **Dangerous distraction.** A distracted Christian is as good as an absent one. Busyness is as good as failure, because it takes us away from the most important focus of keeping our eyes obediently on Jesus.[57] We will spend a great deal more time talking about temptation and misdirection later on, but we must be clear that Satan is content to distract us from our goals.
- **Trial and testing.** For whatever reason, God allows Satan to test believers and nonbelievers by putting them through trials and hardship. (Think of Job's story.) Whether Satan causes trouble, walks us into trouble, or is our trouble, he pushes us to our limits. It seems that God sometimes uses trials to purify us and other times to reveal something that is amiss in our lives, but either way, standing pure and focused under extreme hardship is incredibly difficult. Satan seeks to sift us like wheat, even those who are closest to Jesus—such as one of His best friends, Peter.[58]
- **Divide and conquer.** Predators in the animal kingdom cut off an animal from its herd for attack, and the Devil does the same thing with spiritual attack. Together Christians are mighty; apart we are more vulnerable. Unified we are like a bonfire; apart we are like a fragile match. Because of this, Satan's team spends much of their time trying to instill dissension and disunity into the family of God.[59]

The Father of Lies

I want to spend the remainder of our time talking about the most common strategy that Satan employs in his attempts to destroy us: deception. I want to dig into his nature as a liar, manipulator, counterfeiter, and deceiver. It's Satan's deceptive nature that is our biggest barrier to developing the Master's Mind. We're seeking truth in the way we think about ourselves and the world, but he is actively telling us lies.

Jesus had a tense argument with the religious leaders of His day who opposed Him and denied both His claim to be the Messiah and His teachings. They opposed God to such a degree that He called them children of the Devil·

> You are of *your father the devil,* and your will is to do *your father's desires.* He was a murderer from the beginning, and does not stand in the truth, because *there is no truth in him. When he lies, he speaks out of his own character, for he is a liar and the father of lies.* But because I tell the truth, you do not believe me. (John 8:44–45)

Jesus called the Devil not only a liar but also "the father of lies."

Merriam-Webster defines *lying* as "to make an untrue statement with intent to deceive or to create a false or misleading impression."[60] Lying is all about deception, about distorting the truth to lead someone astray. It is no wonder that Satan is the master of deception; it's in his very nature. In the garden of Eden, at the foot of the Tree of the Knowledge of Good and Evil, he deceived Eve into eating the forbidden fruit.[61] And the lies just kept flowing, as we see all the way through the Bible from the first book to the last. In Revelation 20:10 we read about Satan's end: "The devil who had deceived them was thrown into the lake of fire." Those he leads are cast in the same shadow and model the same behavior.[62]

Lying is about manipulating a person's mind with misleading facts. It's altering the truth to create a new reality. Everything about lying has to do with distorting someone's mind-set and thoughts. Consider the following passages written by the apostle Paul about the wiles of the Devil:

> I am afraid that as the serpent deceived Eve by his cunning, your thoughts will be led astray from a sincere and pure devotion to Christ. (2 Cor. 11:3)

> *The god of this world has blinded the minds of the unbelievers, to keep them from seeing the light of the gospel* of the glory of Christ, who is the image of God. (2 Cor. 4:4)

We see that Satan uses his brilliance either to lead people astray or to block them entirely from seeing another point of view. He is crafty. He knows how to adjust even the littlest bit of information to change the discussion and how to contort the information to lead the witness.

There are many ways to lie. Commonly we think of blatant lies and seemingly innocent "white" lies, but there are innumerable ways to deceive someone. Let's consider one of Satan's favorites.

Counterfeiter

To *counterfeit* is "to imitate something else with the intent to deceive,"[63] and surely the Devil does that.

> For such men are false apostles, deceitful workmen, disguising themselves as apostles of Christ. And no wonder, for *even Satan*

disguises himself as an angel of light. So it is no surprise if *his servants, also, disguise themselves as servants of righteousness.* Their end will correspond to their deeds. (2 Cor. 11:13–15)

Satan pretends to be someone and something he is not so he can get what he wants. (For example, he pretended to be a helpful serpent in the garden so he could encourage Eve to sin.) He is not a creator but a distorter. He will dress himself as a good guy to earn trust, but he is nothing more than a wolf in sheep's clothing. At times in Scripture we even see him counterfeiting miracles to convince people to follow his way[64] or copying God's methods because he's not original enough to make his own ways.[65]

Take, for example, the story of the ten plagues of Egypt.[66] God selected Moses and his brother, Aaron, to represent Him to Pharaoh and ask for the release of the Hebrew slaves. Knowing that Pharaoh would refuse, God enabled Moses to perform a series of miracles—not only to convince Pharaoh to let the people go, but ultimately to bring judgment on the nation of Egypt. At the first meeting where Pharaoh demanded proof of his supernatural authority, Moses broke out his first miracle: he threw down his staff, and it turned into a snake. What is shocking is that Pharaoh called upon his magicians of the black arts and they were able to do the same miracle, turning their staffs into snakes as well.[67] They duplicated the next two miracles too: turning water to blood and calling frogs from the Nile. We see Satan again and again copying the ways of the Lord in order to deceive.

What are some ways that Satan counterfeits to deceive us and to distort our thoughts today?

- Bringing to prominence charismatic leaders who purport to be harbingers of truth when in fact they are either snake-oil salesmen or cult leaders in training

- Introducing us to people who seem to be breaths of fresh air, so we overlook the red flags that point to things that will steal our hearts and crush our souls
- Giving us just enough truth so that we swallow the lie
- Loving us just enough that we accept the abuse
- Promising power but making us puppets
- Luring us with stories about providing for our family, then trapping us in workaholism
- Ensuring us freedom that really leads through a cell door

Why Is He Still Here?

We know the ways Satan tries to deceive us have an effect on how we view ourselves and how we think. So at some point we have to ask the obvious question: If Satan is so wicked and his work is so damaging, why is he still here? Couldn't God have just wiped him out? Surely the Lord is capable of defeating His enemies once and for all, right? We know Satan can't stand against God. We know the Devil is a created being. We know God could crush him at a moment's notice. So why is he still allowed to wreak such havoc?

I've done live Q & A sessions for decades, and I'm consistently asked the question about the Devil's continued existence. It's not only a fair question; it's a brilliant question. Ironically, it has a simple answer: Satan isn't gone because God is still using him. He's a pawn in God's greater strategy. The second God no longer has use for him, he'll be gone. The final chapter has been designed and set. God has already called His shots. In the end, God will shut down the Enemy's plans and throw him and his team in the lake of fire to be tormented forever. But for now, he's still helpful.

In what way?

The most significant role that Satan plays in God's plans seems to be "the other guy." He's the other choice. He's the other pathway. He's the other love. He's the presenter of other options. For whatever reason and by whatever means, God has given us free will to choose whom we love. God wants us to choose Him, but to truly choose someone you need another option. Satan provides that option. To God's truth, he's the lie. To God's obedience, he's the rebellion. To God's calling, he's the carnival barker. To God's bridegroom, he's the adulterous lover.

God also uses Satan for correction. This gets complicated, so let me see if I can simplify it. Satan wants to tear mankind apart, but God won't let him. God keeps Satan on a tether; he is only allowed to do what God permits. Yet if you have a vicious dog straining at the leash and you need someone to be chased down, you let the dog go. Sometimes God uses Satan for judgment, sometimes for discipline, sometimes for execution, sometimes for revealing someone's true nature through testing, sometimes for harassment, and sometimes just to bring humility.[68]

This is why trials and temptations are said to have been sent sometimes by God and sometimes by Satan.[69] The difference is motive.[70]

I don't know whether the Lord reveals His plans to Satan or whether He keeps the Devil in the dark. Either way, God's will is done. Reflect on these examples:

- Jesus was always going to be betrayed into the hands of the authorities so that He might go to the cross and die for the sins of mankind. Satan entered into Judas to make him a betrayer.
- God was always going to demonstrate His full love for mankind through redemption, which required the fall. Satan orchestrated the fall.

When Satan seeks to tear us down, God uses the opportunity to strengthen our faith—which tends to embarrass the Enemy and significantly decrease his impact against the kingdom. The deal doesn't work out well for the Devil, but then again, that's God's plan. God is always ten steps ahead.

Let me be clear on one point: God and Satan are not in cahoots, they are not partners, and they are not on the same team playing different roles. Satan is an enemy of God and is being used for God's purposes. God is not the author of evil, nor does He tempt people.[71] God is crushing Satan little by little until He finishes the job at the end of time. Jesus' kingdom is pressing in, and tension is rising between the realms.

This Means War

We are not only caught in a battle; we are active participants in it. Christ has won the ultimate war, but the struggles continue as the cleanup mission moves forward. Despite Christ's domination, the Enemy bites and claws every day to hang on to his territory, and he's looking for every opportunity to retake what's been purchased for us. Yet we are the soldiers of the Lord's kingdom. The battle is run through His power, His enabling, His plan, and His strategy, but we are a big part of it.

Thankfully, we are not alone. We have monumental help. The assistance is so substantial that it's almost hard to tell what we actually contribute to the war besides merely being a conduit of the heavens. We have at least the following extraordinary help:

- **The Father's Help.** The Father created us to be with Him. He sent His Son to free us and determined that the church would be His bride. He leads the charge to bring us back to

Him in all ways, including protection, guidance, provision, and enablement.[72]

- **King Jesus' Help.** Jesus died to defeat the power of the Devil and death. He has given His all for our freedom and will continue to give more, including intercession, protection, power, and redemption.[73]
- **The Holy Spirit's Help.** The Holy Spirit is the primary Person of the Godhead working with the church today. He is the active bodyguard, expeller of demons, and deliverer of those He loves. His work includes protection, power, presence, peace, and instruction.[74]
- **Angelic Help.** The biblical term for *angel* includes all types of heavenly host: cherubim, seraphim, angels, archangels, and others.[75] The Bible says that their primary purpose is to carry out the will of God in ministry to us. We have an angelic host watching over us and taking care of us.

Authority and Power

Not only are we on the winning side, helped by the heavenly host and securely in the territory owned by the kingdom of light, but God has also enlisted us into His army and endowed us with the authority and power to defeat the works of the Enemy when necessary. Jesus said to His disciples, beginning with Peter but including them all,

> And I tell you, you are Peter, and *on this rock I will build my church, and the gates of hell shall not prevail against it. I will give you the keys of the kingdom* of heaven, and whatever you bind on earth shall be bound in heaven, and whatever you loose on earth shall be loosed in heaven. (Matt. 16:18–19)

Jesus' promise was confirmed in their ministry:

> The seventy-two returned with joy, saying, *"Lord, even the demons are subject to us in your name!"* And *he said* to them, *"I saw Satan fall like lightning from heaven. Behold, I have given you authority* to tread on serpents and scorpions, *and over all the power of the enemy*, and nothing shall hurt you. Nevertheless, do not rejoice in this, that *the spirits are subject to you*, but rejoice that your names are written in heaven." (Luke 10:17–20)

And it was passed to us:

> For *the weapons of our warfare are not of the flesh but have divine power to destroy strongholds.* We destroy arguments and every lofty opinion raised against the knowledge of God, and take every thought captive to obey Christ, being ready to punish every disobedience, when your obedience is complete. (2 Cor. 10:4–6)[76]

"Divine power to destroy strongholds." Let that resound in your soul. Divine power, from God—the same power that raised Jesus from the dead[77]—is available to us for spiritual victory over the Enemy and his lies. We use it "to destroy strongholds . . . arguments . . . lofty opinion," and to "take every thought captive to obey Christ." Whatever the Enemy throws at us or whatever territory he has stolen from us, by the power of Jesus Christ we can retake it and master it.

It's important to note that our authority is based on who we are, not on what we have done. We are children of God because of what He has done. This means that we have the rights of the royal family. We are free and able to authorize commands of the kingdom. The

Enemy knows that to mess with us is to mess with the entire force of heaven. Collectively we are the bride of Christ; individually we are princes and princesses of the realm.

Our power is based on our authority. When God gave us the right to command His will on His behalf, it came with inherent power. The Bible tells us that the name of the Lord Jesus Christ is incredibly powerful. We operate in that name. At the name of Jesus Christ every knee will bow and every tongue confess that He is Lord. The demons know that now; the world will know that later. We are empowered to carry out the call of God and defeat the Enemy when he stands against it.

It's time that we make Satan pay for harming the body of Christ. Next time he tempts or hurts someone we love, we should retaliate by praying extra hard that the Lord would humble him and knock him down even more. For every square inch that he gains in our minds, hearts, and lives, we should take back an acre of his territory. As he has tried to master our minds for his deluded purposes, we must use the Lord's authority and power to reclaim our thoughts, begin to discipline and purify them as their rightful masters, and submit them to our Lord and Master for His glory! It's time to show the Enemy who is the real master of our minds.

Chapter 4

Temptation ~~Island~~ Desert

For us to master our minds, we must deal with the issue of sin. Sin takes us from where we should be to where we should not be. Sin turns us from God's best. Sin ruins our thoughts and poisons our hearts. Sin stands in the way of a well-ordered, God-honoring mind. Ironically, we sin because our minds are askew, and our minds are askew because of sin.

But sin may not be what we think it is.

Sin is that which God is not. It's the antithesis of His nature—anything un-Godlike. Sin is godlessness. It's a mode of being, an attitude, a state of mind.

The Bible has a few different words for sin. Two of the most common are translated as *transgression* (in Greek, *parabasis*) and *missed the mark* (in Greek, *hamartia*). *Transgression* means knowingly or unknowingly crossing a line. There was a definite boundary and, despite warnings, we walked past it. A transgression is a violation. *Missing the mark* means that there was a bull's-eye—an expectation or a demand we were aiming for—and we missed it. God's nature is perfect, but our response was imperfect.

What's shocking to some is that the penalty for both transgression and missing the mark is death. Romans 6:23 says, "The wages of sin is death." In other words, the payment required for violating God's nature is punishment and permanent removal from His presence. Yikes! That's why Jesus had to rescue us and why God treats sin like such a big deal.

Why such a severe judgment? A violation against a created thing is significant, but a violation against an infinite God is unacceptable. God is holy, righteous, and the cause of all life. He is not merely another sinful creation who is morally on par with us.

If we remember that sin is anti-God, we can see how God cannot and will not tolerate it. Sin is rebellion, whether or not we knew it to be. Our sinful choices deserve punishment; our sinful nature demands destruction. It's not about God not being forgiving or understanding; it's more about us defying our created intent. We were built to be with God and for God, but if sin has left us in a state where we cannot be with Him or for Him, then we cease to purposefully exist.

Sin is such a big deal to God because it is contrary to His nature and His best. God is all that is good; therefore, sin is always not good. God is all that is healthy and whole; therefore, sin is unhealthy and dysfunctional. God is loving and kind; therefore, sin is selfish and evil.

Temptation is any voice that calls us away from God and His way. Temptation baits us to commit sinful acts, acts that are harmful, dangerous, and thereby condemned by God. So why would we fall for it? Why would a good-hearted Christian struggle with sin at all if we love God and sin is anti-God?

My favorite practical definition of a sinful act is "the meeting of legitimate needs by illegitimate means." In other words, sin is feeding a real craving with a harmful solution—so temptation is anything that encourages us to use the illegitimate, harmful means.

Temptation itself is not sin, but it leads to sin. Temptation is the lure, the whisper, the pressure, the suggestion, the pull to something other than what God wants. I like to think of temptation as proverbial junk food or a shortcut. When we're hungry, the healthiest thing is a balanced meal, but the easiest thing is a Twinkie. The right way to run a race is the long way around, but the fastest way is to take a shortcut. Temptation, in a sense, is the wrong way to do the right thing. And we have a lot of opportunities to do things the wrong way.

Although everyone is continually tempted, not all temptations look the same. What tempts one person may not tempt another. We need to ask ourselves some questions: What feeling does temptation elicit in us? What is stirring in our emotions when we're tempted? Can we identify that craving or need that we are trying to meet?

Whether we're facing the flesh, the world, or the Devil, temptation seems to be the primary challenge that provides a doorway for sin and prevents us from keeping our minds aligned with the Lord. And temptation is a prime example of how powerful our minds are, as it happens in the mind long before we act on it. So our minds must be ready to resist it. We need to know who we are in Christ and what we're here to do, not be distracted by other ideas about our identities and callings. We need to keep our minds fixed on what is true, not believe Satan's lies, the distortions of the world, or the cravings of the flesh. We need the Master's Mind.

We'll talk more about resisting temptation in the next chapter, but here we'll examine some common temptations we face and the distorted mind-sets they reveal. Then we'll take a look at Jesus' example of faithfulness in temptation.

Unsurprisingly, the same three thieves that try to steal our identities are also the sources of temptation: the world around us, the flesh within us, and the Devil coming after us. Each is trying to pull us away from God and to keep us from knowing our identity. They try to distort our thoughts, so our job is to keep our minds strong and focused on who God is, who we are in light of Him, and what's true.

Temptations from the World

Earlier I defined *the world* as the non-God part of our society. Now let me be clear: our society has plenty of wonderful parts that God has breathed life into and that display His beauty. I am a firm believer that all that is incredible in history—brilliance, prodigy, creativity, power, leadership, art, music, literature, and the like—began as the direct influence and gifting of God. Here, however, I am going to focus on those parts of our culture that are anti-God.

Our world is filled with messages that completely contradict the truth of Christ, and that is not an accident. Elements of our society have been designed by broken people who are leading and influencing other broken people. Many of these systems and beliefs appear innocent, yet that is what makes them so dangerous. I cannot list them all, so I will highlight a couple of distorted patterns of thinking common in the world today. These distortions tempt us by pulling us away from the truth of who God is and who we are in Him.[1]

More Is Better

Almost every TV commercial preaches the same thing: all you need is more, and if you only had this product, you would be fulfilled. These are lies. More is not always better, and genuine satisfaction comes only from doing things God's way. Anyone with wisdom knows that the answer to the question "How much is enough?" is always "Just a little bit more." We are never satisfied. No matter how much we get, we want more. Our bodies are designed on the circular concept of need, satiation, more need. We eat and get full, and then hours later we are hungry again. We drink glasses of water only to be thirsty again. We sleep eight hours and have to do it again the next night. This is the way God designed us when it comes to our basic needs. But we've taken it further, to our wants. We get a new toy, are quickly bored with it, and want a different one. It's been the same since we were toddlers.

We have the same reaction when it comes to sex or money—we have a perpetual drive for more. Yet even the people the world considers the sexiest rarely seem satisfied with their relationships, and even some millionaires live paycheck to paycheck, spending above their means and continually wanting more. But if the wealthiest of us continue to crave, what hope do we have of satiation? The "more is better" mind set is a lie.

Satisfaction Is Possible

The lie corresponding to "more is better" is that satisfaction is possible and fulfillment is right around the corner. We are taught that at the end of the rainbow is a pot of gold, only to discover that no matter how far we go, the rainbow never gets any closer. Commercials show that other people are happy and satisfied, so what's wrong with us? If we have unmet needs, we assume something is wrong. We think we are missing something, so we go on an eternal quest for satisfaction, only to learn that it doesn't exist. It was never meant to in this world.

We lost satisfaction when Eve took the forbidden fruit, and we won't get it back until sin is finally removed and we are transferred to heaven in our glorified bodies. God's presence is the only thing that will ever satisfy us. While we get glimpses of it on this sin-polluted earth, we won't ever fully experience it until we are purified and with Him one day in heaven. Until then we'll find no fulfillment—not today, not tomorrow.

Contentment is different from satisfaction, and it's something we can experience now. Contentment means that we don't have to continually look for more; we can decide that we have enough. When we're content, we realize we aren't going to be satisfied, and we are okay with that. The more content we are with how God's already blessed us, the less power Satan has over us. It's our job to be "filled up" in God so that we can stand.

The apostle Paul wrote:

> But *godliness with contentment* is great gain, for we brought nothing into the world, and we cannot take anything out of the world. But if we have food and clothing, with *these we will be content. But those who desire to be rich fall into temptation,* into a snare, into many senseless and harmful desires that plunge people into ruin and destruction. For *the love of money is a root of all kinds of evils. It is through this craving that some have wandered away from the faith and pierced themselves with many pangs.* (1 Tim. 6:6–10)[2]

If we think we always need more, we'll be tempted to do all kinds of wrong things to get what we believe we deserve. But when we remember that true satisfaction comes only from God, we'll be able to be content—and the world's temptations won't have as much power over us.

Temptations of the Flesh

Remember that the flesh is the part of us that is not yet surrendered to Jesus Christ. It's the bad part of us—the sin part[3] and the selfish part that struggles to submit to any type of rule. The flesh resists good and fights for supremacy. Selfishness is at the heart of temptations of the flesh. I already mentioned the most obvious one—sex—but here are a few others.

Pride

Pride is being impressed with ourselves and thinking about ourselves too much. The opposite of pride is humility, which doesn't mean thinking less *of* oneself, but thinking less *about* oneself. Pride is thinking we are more important than others; it creates a hierarchy of people over which we become king. Few sins stir God's ire more than pride, because acting pridefully is essentially calling ourselves gods. Pride is the temptation to think that we have risen above everyone else and deserve special treatment.

Allowing pride to take root in our lives distorts the very order of creation. We no longer allow God to be God, and we don't partner with the rest of creation in the interdependence He intended. We cease to properly respect those around us, and we fall prey to believing that all things exist for our own well-being. Pride is the most foolish of all sins, because it defies all the facts before us. With our limitations, we cannot be gods. We cannot be greater than other humans who were also created in God's image. We cannot do anything about our fragility, our afterlife, our ultimate health, or our most important relationships. Any honest evaluation of a human life must come to the conclusion that we are merely jars of clay. Yet the temptation to pride persists.

Self-Obsession

Similar to pride is the temptation of self-obsession, which causes us to stop thinking about others altogether. We simply think about ourselves, what we want, what we need, what we like and don't like. This turns us into monsters of consumption. If we are the only people in the universe, then all things must exist for our appetites—and that includes other people.

It's evil to use up the resources around us, leaving none for others, but it's even more evil to become so selfish that we use people for our own desires. Once we cross the line of self-obsession, or extreme selfishness, suddenly other people become a means to an end. If we want attention, we will do whatever it takes to get it—and then discard the relationship when it ceases to feed our ego. If we want our cravings fed, we'll use anyone to stuff the void. If we seek power, we will step on anyone to climb the ladder of influence. Once people have become consumable, we have lost our way.

The distorted mind-set of the flesh leads us to believe we are the most important. When we think that way, we're tempted to treat others terribly. We need to remember that God is the King; we are not. When we have that mind-set, we know we are valuable because of our relationship with Him, but we are not more valuable than His other children.

Temptation from the Devil: Distortion Through Doubt

We've already talked extensively about the father of lies, so I'll mention only one more of his temptations here: distortion through doubt.

One of the Devil's sneakiest tricks is causing us to doubt the goodness and truth of God.

Satan took this approach with Eve. Instead of a frontal assault, he slithered up next to her in the garden of Eden and began to ask her questions. "Did God actually say, 'You shall not eat of any tree in the garden?'" (Gen. 3:1). He caused her to question God's rules and heart.

When Eve's conscience kicked in, she tried to fend Satan off and return to what she knew of God by saying that His guideline was for her protection—that if she ate of the fruit, she would die. And here the serpent's brilliance showed most brightly: "You will not surely die," he hissed (Gen. 3:4).

And he was right—kind of.

That's the beauty of this type of deception: it's partially right but leads someone to take it further. Satan was correct; Eve would not die immediately from eating the fruit, at least not physically. But he didn't happen to mention that God was talking about spiritual death. He didn't mention that even though Adam and Eve wouldn't feel the consequences immediately, they were nevertheless true. He didn't mention that God is always right. He simply asked a question, and Eve's mind and heart did the rest.

She wondered: Was God holding out on her? Did God really intend the best for her and her husband? Was there more to life? Was she missing out?

How many of these questions has Satan gotten you to swallow? I've bought them all at times. One question leads to another. One doubt leads to another. In the end we are further from our Lord than when we began.[4]

Here are some of the most common modern-day questions the Devil uses to get us to doubt God or lead us down the wrong path:

- Would God really want you to suffer like that?
- Why is God against fun?
- Does God really appreciate all that you've done for Him?
- Why do other people seem to be having all the fun?
- Who's going to know?
- Isn't there an easier way to do this?
- Why would a good God treat you like a servant when you were made to be powerful?
- Would God really be so single-minded as to make only one way to heaven?

And we take it from there.

The Devil tempts us to doubt God's goodness, to assume that He isn't looking out for us so we need to look out for ourselves.

That faulty mind-set leads us into all kinds of disobedience and takes us away from God's best for us. But when we remember the truth about God—that He made us, that He loves us, that He sacrificed Himself for us—we have an easier time following Him.

Jesus in the Desert

Let me state the obvious: the key to battling temptation is to follow the example of Christ.

Thankfully, the Bible gives us at least one full account of how Jesus dealt with significant temptation. Jesus did not have an easy, trouble-free life. Hebrews 4:15, speaking of Jesus' wrestling with temptation, says, "We do not have a high priest who is unable to *sympathize with our weaknesses,* but one who *in every respect has been tempted as we are,* yet without sin."[5] And not only has He been tempted in every respect, but it cost Him. The author of Hebrews also wrote, "For because *he himself has suffered when tempted,* he is able to help those who are being tempted" (Heb. 2:18). Jesus struggled through temptation as we do. Sure, He started with a clean slate (He didn't have an original sin nature, unlike us), but He still knows what temptation is like and how hard it is to resist.

Let's take a look at the most significant recorded temptations of Christ. I will give a combined account from three gospel passages:

> **And then Jesus, full of the Holy Spirit, returned from the Jordan and *immediately* was led up (and) *(driven)* by the Spirit *out into* the wilderness for forty days, to be tempted by the devil. He ate nothing during those days *and he was with the wild animals*. And after fasting forty days and forty nights, he was hungry. And the tempter *(Satan)* came, the devil, and said to him, "*If you are the Son of God, command these stones to become loaves of bread."* But Jesus answered him, "It is**

written, 'Man shall not live by bread alone, <u>but by every word that comes from the mouth of God.</u>'" And <u>again,</u> the devil took him up <u>to a very high mountain</u> and showed him all the kingdoms of the world <u>and their glory</u> in a moment of time, and <u>he</u> said to him, *"To you I will give all this authority, all these and their glory, for it has been delivered to me, and I give it to whom I will. If you, then, will <u>fall down</u> <u>and</u> worship me, it will all be yours."* And Jesus answered him, "It is written, 'You shall worship the Lord your God, and him only shall you serve.'" <u>Then the devil</u> took him to <u>the holy city,</u> Jerusalem and set him on the pinnacle of the temple and said to him, *"If you are the Son of God, throw yourself down from here, for it is written, 'He will command his angels concerning you, to guard you,' and 'On their hands they will bear you up, lest you strike your foot against a stone.'"* And Jesus answered him, "<u>Again</u> it is said/ <u>written,</u> 'You shall not put the Lord your God to the test.'" And when the devil had ended every temptation, <u>Jesus said to him, "Be gone, Satan!"</u> Then the devil departed from him until an opportune time <u>and behold,</u> *the* <u>angels came and were ministering to him.</u> And Jesus returned in the power of the Spirit to Galilee, and a report about him went out through all the surrounding country. And he taught in their synagogues, being glorified by all.[*]

Although we could look at this story a hundred different ways, I want to spend the majority of our time understanding how the temptations challenged Jesus' identity and way of thinking. In essence, the Devil brought three temptations against Christ, and they bear some similarities to the ones we just talked about: (1) the

---

[*] This passage has been paraphrased from Matt. 4:1–11 (underlined text); Mark 1:12–13 (bold italic text); Luke 4:1–15 (bold text).

temptation of appetite, (2) the temptation of ambition, and (3) the temptation of approval or arrogance.

Appetite

"If you are the Son of God, command these stones to become loaves of bread."

The Devil tempted Jesus with a single sentence. But what's wrong with making something to eat? What's wrong with Jesus showing His identity as Son of God by meeting a very real need? The Devil is in the details.

Satan was tempting Jesus to feed Himself and cut out God. At a deeper level, this was a temptation for Christ to doubt the provision of a good God, act independently of the Father, and fix His situation without submitting to it as the Father had designed. The Devil pointed out that because Jesus was the Son of God, He had power at His disposal to fix His discomfort—and argued that He should utilize it. The act of turning something into bread was not a sin (later Jesus did a lot with bread); the temptation was in the timing. The Father wanted Jesus to be hungry. The Spirit had brought Jesus out to the wilderness for a time of deliberate extended fasting and prayer, so satisfying His hunger would be defying the will of the Father. At its core, this was a test of who was running the agenda—self or God?

With one statement, the Devil tried to get Jesus to doubt God's goodness. He even implied that since Jesus was the Son of God, He should be treated better.

As hard as it might be for us to believe, the Father's will was for Jesus to suffer. I think this is where we often get it wrong. We think that God always wants us to be content, comfortable, easy, and relaxed, and anything that makes us feel differently should be removed from our lives. But that's simply not true. The Father was strengthening His Son and revealing His character through the suffering. The Father didn't want the trial of hunger solved. He wanted the difficulty to remain, and the temptation was to make it easy again.[6]

Most of the sins I suffer from are pacifiers trying to compensate for my distorted appetite for comfort. Instead of walking through a challenge, we numb ourselves to it. Whether it's by zoning out with TV, reading a book, drinking alcohol, viewing porn, surfing the Internet, doing drugs, getting attention, or finding something else that soothes our minds, we do everything we can to avoid feeling the pain. The world around us says we shouldn't experience discomfort in any way, and if we do, something is wrong and should be corrected. But any padding we put on that allows us not to rely on Jesus Christ becomes sin for us. We're counting on something else, someone else, to take care of our needs, even though God may want to use discomfort to teach us.

Our temptation is to worry that God is not good and doesn't want what's best for us, and believing that leads us down bad paths.

Ambition

"Bow down to me and I'll give you what you want."

Temptations involving ambition are sneaky because Satan doesn't need us to want something bad. He can work just as well with us wanting something good. Jesus wanted a lot of good things: He wanted to follow His Father's will and save His people from their sins. He wanted to advance His kingdom on earth and defeat the Devil. He wanted to control the outcomes of all those He loved so desperately. He wanted to protect us.

Satan knew Jesus' desires, wants, motivations, and dreams. He was offering Jesus a shortcut, and therein lay the temptation. Remember, Satan's most common trick is to tempt us to fill a legitimate need by illegitimate means. When he offered the world to Jesus, it was a temptation to get the kingdom and avoid the cross.

It involved eroding what was best into what was mediocre or dangerous. He does this with us, too, telling us, "Let's not do it God's way—that's too hard. There's an easier way." The temptation of ambition is about compromising with evil to get "good stuff" accomplished. It's cutting corners. It's the temptation not to wait and follow God's methods but instead to get something done through our own wisdom and smarts.

The Father had already revealed that Jesus was going to be given the world's kingdom. The question was, which method would get Him there? That's where Satan struck. Jesus knew He had supernatural powers. What was He going to do with them? Use them for Himself or submit them to the Father for His purposes?

Satan's offer of the world was legitimate,[7] but had Jesus accepted the offer, all that He stood for would have failed. To bow to Satan in any way was to lose everything that mattered. The whole point of Christ's life on earth was to live in submission to the Father, not to anyone else. Satan knew that to get Jesus to submit was to get supreme authority, far greater than dominion over the world. Jesus was not only sharp enough to pick up on that, but His heart was pure and determined enough to follow His Father's agenda and stand against the temptation. If Jesus had been after mere power and authority, He might have fallen for this offer. But He had a different priority.

Arrogance and Approval

"If you are the Son of God, throw yourself down from here."

Jump off a ledge and God will save you—that's a temptation? Scholars debate what this temptation was really about. Some say that Jesus was being tempted to demonstrate His power to an audience. The reasoning goes like this: The temple was one of the most crowded places in Jerusalem. Imagine if Jesus went up to a pinnacle, high above the temple square where everyone could see

Him. If He jumped down and suddenly angels came, swept Him up in their arms, and rested Him safely on the ground, everyone would know that there was a new sheriff in town. Just like that, Jesus would have credibility, fame, and authority. I call this the temptation of arrogance, because it hinges on the desire to be set apart and gain attention.

Another possibility is that this was the temptation of approval. Maybe Jesus wanted to know if people would approve of His leadership. Maybe He desperately wanted another affirmation from His heavenly Father, confirming that He was chosen and protected. Or maybe Jesus just wanted other people to approve His plan of going into public ministry and knew He could achieve that by impressing them with His Father's miraculous rescue.[8]

We fall into traps of both approval and arrogance, and they seem to be variations of one another. Whether it's an obvious demand for God to expose His value and power, or a subtle cry for approval, each is an attempt to manipulate God to act. Although it's natural to desire approval, there are right and wrong ways to get what we want.

Testing God usually means challenging Him defiantly, forcing God to prove again that He is powerful, righteous, and a good provider. The appropriate response for God's people is to wait patiently on the Lord and His provision, in His time, following His direction. Ultimately, testing God is about doubting Him and trying to make Him prove Himself. Jesus demonstrated that He didn't need any tests to prove the goodness of the Father. He lived by faith alone and trusted that His Lord is good.

Any time we demand something from God, it comes from a place of arrogance, whether we know it or not. When we scream at God that our cancer struggle is unfair, we are subtly trying to control God as if we knew what is best.[9] To a more blatant degree, when we demand that God prove Himself, we are believing in our hearts that we have the right to do that, that we are the boss and commander. We are not. Satan knows that pride distances us from the Lord, so the more we inject selfish modes of thinking into our minds, the better for him.

In a sense, this set of three temptations asked a very important question of Jesus: *What type of Messiah are You going to be?* Christ was fully human as well as fully divine, and although God had already revealed that His calling was to be the promised Messiah, this process of *becoming* Messiah, Savior, and Leader was all new. He, like all Jews, had some idea of who the Messiah should be, but how would He do it? Would He go the traditional route of impressing people through signs and wonders? Would He use power and force? Would He lead a rebellion against Rome, like the Jews wanted? Or would He do what He sensed He was being called to do, which was to take the Suffering Servant role? Doing that would result in being continually questioned and doubted. It was a pathway most people wouldn't understand, and, consequently, He would not often be praised or encouraged.

Through Christ's humanity, Satan was trying to get a foothold to tempt Him to become the Messiah in a more "efficient" manner that would allegedly work for both Him and the Father. Christ refused this and humbly submitted to His heavenly Father, accepting only His directions. Christ was learning by doing, and through His humanity He became perfect through suffering[10]— meaning that He was proven to be the sinless Lamb of God, an appropriate sacrifice for the sins of the world.

What Christ's Victory Over Temptation Teaches Us

The desert temptations were an incredible opportunity for Christ to be the perfect representative of humanity. They were an opportunity to redo the garden of Eden temptation and the wilderness wandering of Israel, and a chance to demonstrate to the Devil what a true, obedient servant looks like. Jesus' responses showed God's kids how a faithful child of God lives.

Jesus Showed Obedience

Jesus didn't try to outsmart the Devil or come up with a brilliant new plan. Jesus just did what His Father wanted Him to—and that is our job too. Instead of trying harder to fight against the temptation or maneuver through it, we are called to obey. God knows where the temptation comes from, how it's designed, and how we can find the way out. Our goal is to close our eyes and listen. The way out of every temptation is simple to say but harder to live: obedience.

Jesus Is the New Adam

Adam was created in a perfect world, the best version of perfect humanity, with everything he needed, and he failed to resist temptation. Jesus was in a dry, hot, terrible desert with nothing, and He won. The temptations were essentially the same: to doubt God's goodness, and to fix your problem and get what you want through an illegitimate pathway (physical appetite; desire for personal gain; easy path to glory). Adam and Eve caved to those temptations; Jesus did not. Jesus was redeeming the dominion of the earth that Adam and Eve handed over to Satan.[11]

And He did it. He overcame. He demonstrated to all of creation that obedience was more important than everything else and that the world was His. As we obey, a new light of more freedom and more victory dawns in our souls.

Jesus Is the New Israel

In the Bible, God calls Israel both His son and His servant. Israel was designed to display God's nature to the world. The people were supposed to represent God's will to a lost and dying race, and they were called to follow God's every command. And what happened? They failed, but Jesus proved faithful. As God led the Israelites into the desert, the Holy Spirit led Jesus into the desert. This connection is highlighted in the gospel accounts, since all three of Jesus' rebukes to Satan are quotations from Deuteronomy that are specifically about the Israelites' wanderings. Their three tests: (1) Israel was allowed to hunger to show that bread isn't everything; (2) Israel was told to worship God alone and not serve other gods of the nations around them; and (3) Israel was told not to put God to the test by complaining or grumbling. Where they failed, Christ succeeded.

Jesus demonstrated that selfishness and fear do not have to dictate our lives. He displayed God's nature properly to the world. He showed that God's people could follow His every command. He silently and without grumbling walked the road to the cross to worship God alone. He is our example par excellence.

Jesus Is a Glorious Demonstration to the Heavenlies

Knowing the heart of obedience in His one and only Son, Jesus, the Father demonstrated to the angels and demons that the Son was qualified for His messianic mission. Everyone was watching. The Father revealed His greatest servant in Christ! Because of the nature of the Trinity, God already knew Jesus' character, so the temptation didn't reveal anything new to Him. However, it revealed a lot to His creation. In addition, it exposed Satan and his tactics so we have a better chance of resisting them. Jesus' victory got us greater power to have victory. Today we, too, are surrounded by a great cloud of witnesses looking in to see what God has done, is doing, and will do.

Jesus Is a Perfect Example for Us Today

One of the key reasons Christ came to earth was to live a life we could imitate. He became fully human so He could give us a tangible example of how to live in connection with the Father and in the power of the Holy Spirit. We are to fight temptation the way that Jesus did, with absolute obedience and the truth of the Word of God.

I don't think that most temptation should be as difficult as we make it, if we follow Jesus' example.

The more we say yes to God, the easier it is to say yes to Him the next time. The more we lean into healthy patterns of obedience, the more our bodies adjust to that response. With each victory, we struggle to earn in our minds, the next decision is smoother. It's all about habit patterns.

When Jesus walked into the desert, He was in the habit of saying yes to God and no to sin. He had been doing that for thirty years. That doesn't mean it wasn't difficult. It simply means that His body, soul, and spirit were prepped to fight, and He had developed every advantage given to Him by His Father through saying yes over and over again.

We, on the other hand—or maybe I should speak for myself here—haven't established that same pattern. I have said yes to sin and no to God more times than I can count, and Satan knows that. During some seasons of my life, even the slightest proverbial wind of sin could blow me over. I have exercised my sin muscles and played the forgiveness card so often that I have trained myself how to live in sin. Jesus hadn't, and it made all the difference.

But we can change our patterns. The more we say no to sin and yes to God, the more likely we are to overcome temptation the next time. It's like working out at the gym. The stronger our minds become, the more power we have to say no both to ourselves and to our enemies.

All temptation begins in the mind. When we recognize the distorted thought patterns we've talked about in this chapter, we can better recognize them—and we can work on developing the truth-filled mind-sets of the Master, recognizing both who He is and who we really are.

Chapter 5

Arming the Resistance

W e've looked at common temptations and learned from Jesus' example. Before we talk more about how to fight temptation and retake the territory of our minds, let's look briefly at why God allows temptation at all. Why do we have to deal with it, and what does fighting it do for us?

Why God Allows Trial and Temptation

God allows temptation and trial because they can be good for us.

Seriously? Yep.

The same Greek and Hebrew words are used in Scripture for both *temptation* and *trial*. The distinction depends on intent and motivation. Is the difficult situation for the purpose of tearing down? It's a temptation. Is it for the purpose of building up? It's a trial.

Temptation is a lure to sin. God doesn't do that, but He does test.

Blessed is the man who remains steadfast under trial, for when he has stood the test he will receive the crown of life, which God has promised to those who love him. *Let no one say when*

he is tempted, "I am being tempted by God," for God cannot be
tempted with evil, and he himself tempts no one. But each person
is tempted when he is lured and enticed by his own desire. Then
desire when it has conceived gives birth to sin, and sin when it is
fully grown brings forth death. Do not be deceived, my beloved
brothers. Every good gift and every perfect gift is from above,
coming down from the Father of lights with whom there is no
variation or shadow due to change. (James 1:12–17)

Remember, sin is that which is anti-God. Therefore, God will
never lead someone to sin; doing so goes against His very nature.
However, He will test believers by putting them through difficult
training that will both strengthen them and reveal their current
conditions (like a refiner's fire).

Both situations involve challenge. How do we know then if it's
a temptation or a trial? We don't—that's God's business. In either
situation, we are to remain faithful to the Lord and believe He will
reveal the reason in due time. If we are obedient in a temptation,
we will resist the Devil, and he will flee from us. If we're obedient
in a trial, we will emerge stronger than ever. We must believe by
faith that God has our best interests in mind and not doubt His
love or provision regardless of the circumstances we are going
through.

Intent means everything. If I as a leader demanded that my
followers run until they threw up, forced them to work for me
in grueling circumstances to the detriment of their bodies, and
humiliated them continually to destroy their hearts, I would be a
monster. If I did it for their best interests, I would be a drill instruc-
tor. If I rubbed acid on someone's face so that it bubbled and hurt,
and the person had to take meds for weeks just to deal with the
burns I created, I would be a devil. If I did it because the person
asked me to, I would be a dermatologist performing a chemical

peel. If I dropped heavy items on you that could crush you, only to force you to catch them and push them back up, I would be a tormentor. If I did it for the good of your body, I would be a personal trainer in the gym. If I withheld your normal food for days on end and then only gave you small amounts of berries and vegetables even though there was a bounty of food around, you would call me selfish. If I did it for your health, I'd be a nutritionist helping you with a fast or cleanse. As you can see, it's not the brutal situation that makes something good or bad, but the motive behind it. That's also true of troubles in our lives.

If we listen to Satan, we assume the worst of God; if we know who God is, we assume the best—and that changes everything about how we respond. We can know He has a valuable reason for the trials we are facing.

Satan seeks to harm. He wants to take us down. He wants us to turn our back on God[1] and sin.[2] Satan and his demons want to rip our faces off; the only reason they can't do that is because God holds the leash. Why doesn't God stop them completely and keep us safe? Because safe isn't the pathway to either strength or revelation.

God's intention is always for believers to emerge from a trial better than when they started, either in strength or in knowledge. He promises that every situation will have a way out—an escape hatch that can be utilized through obedience.[3] The way out may not be easy, and we may not always take it, but its presence means that we will never be forced to sin. God will never do that.

We will experience temptation, but let me reiterate: temptation isn't sin.

As we've seen, the Bible says that Jesus was tempted yet was without sin.[4] It also says, "In your anger do not sin" (Eph. 4:26 NIV). This means that difficult, messy things are not always sin. Evil may surround us, but we can remain untouched internally, where it matters. Christians deal with too much self-condemnation for being tempted. The reality is that temptation is normal. It doesn't mean we are bad people, only that we are human.

Too many times we think that because we struggle with something, we may as well just cave in. That's a lie from the Enemy. Of course we want to give in; that's what temptation is. But not giving in is what *resistance* is.

When God tests humans, it's always for our best. It was not an accident that the Tree of the Knowledge of Good and Evil was in the middle of the garden of Eden. God could have put it in the far corner, but He placed it squarely in the center so that Adam and Eve would have to walk past it no matter where they were headed. He was helping them develop patterns of obedience, which revealed their love for Him for the supernatural world to see. Did it cost Him? Yes, of course it did. God lost His beautiful intimacy with His brand-new creation. He lost the connection that was the very purpose for mankind's design. But God used even Adam and Eve's failure to demonstrate the most powerful act of love known to mankind: redemption.[5]

An often forgotten verse from the end of Christ's desert temptation is found in Luke 4:14, and it speaks volumes: "And Jesus returned in the power of the Spirit to Galilee."

Jesus came out of the desert trial more powerful than He was before. He underwent temptations at the beginning of His public ministry so that His power would be present for His work. Obedience results in power. When we emerge from a trial successfully, not only is God glorified, but also we are strengthened in confidence and in the certainty of God's will for our lives. The Holy Spirit comes in and fills that empty spot (where we empty ourselves of our pride, our needs, our cravings, or our agendas) with Himself, and we are empowered even more. God brings trials to our lives for this outcome.

Temptations provide an opportunity for us to strengthen our faith, learn significant lessons, and honor God, but we need to learn some strategies for that to happen. God has given us more than enough power and plenty of authority. He has exposed many of the Devil's tricks in Scripture. He has provided truth to sharpen our minds as well as instruction on how to honor Him. Let's take a look at a few of the tools the Lord has given us.

How Do We Fight Back?

Standing Our Ground

Christians stand on holy ground. When Christ said, "It is finished" with His last breaths on the cross, He delivered the fatal blow to the Devil.[6] He rescued us from the kingdom of darkness and placed us firmly in the kingdom of light.[7] Jesus soundly defeated the power of the Enemy,[8] and although He is still actively leading a charge to shut down all rebellious activity, He reigns.[9] This means that God has already won and continues to win.

So many spiritual warfare passages in the Bible tell us to stand and watch God win.[10] At times we are called to engage on His behalf, but most of the time we are simply told to stand, because He has already taken the territory of our hearts and minds.

Remember when Moses led the Hebrew people out of Egypt, and God led them to the edge of the Red Sea? Blocked in the front with the pursuing Egyptian army behind, they panicked and cried out for Moses to do something. Instead of coming up with another brilliant evasion strategy, Moses had the wisdom and connection with God to know that the Lord had another plan, a plan to fight for Israel Himself and give the people a front-row seat for His victory over their enemies: "Moses said to the people, *'Fear not, stand firm*, and see the salvation of the LORD, which *he will work for you today.* For the Egyptians whom you see today, you shall never see

again. *The* LORD *will fight for you, and you have only to be silent'"*
(Ex. 14:13–14).

When it comes to the territory of our minds, God often tells
us to be still and let Him fight for us. He has brought defeat to the
Enemy many times, and we need only to receive His freedom and
not return to distorted thinking.[11]

At other times, we are called to actively resist. After we watch
God set us free, it's our job to hold that new ground and not let it be
retaken by the Enemy. We have something he wants, and over and
over we are told to resist him. We aren't trying to take anything
from him; he's trying to take it from us.[12] He wants everything he
can get that Jesus bought for us, including our freedom—but we
don't need to fear.

We are not fighting a losing battle. Our Master has taken and
established the land of our minds. They are ultimately His; therefore, the Enemy knows he is working from a losing position. If
we're Christians, Satan can only occupy parts of our minds tem-
porarily if we let him. And we don't fight alone. God is fighting
for us, and He will win—there's no question. In the meantime, He
gives us everything we need for victory.

Armor of God

One of the precious tools God has provided is supernatural
protection for His children. The apostle Paul called it the armor
of God:

> *Put on the whole armor of God, that you may be able to stand*
> against the schemes of the devil. For we do not wrestle against
> flesh and blood, but *against the rulers, against the authorities,*
> *against the cosmic powers over this present darkness, against the*
> *spiritual forces of evil in the heavenly places.* Therefore *take up the*
> *whole armor of God, that you may be able to withstand* in the evil

day, and having done all, to *stand firm. Stand* therefore, having fastened on the *belt of truth,* and having put on the *breastplate of righteousness,* and, as *shoes* for your feet, having put on *the readiness given by the gospel of peace.* In all circumstances take up the *shield of faith,* with which you can extinguish all the flaming darts of the evil one; and take the *helmet of salvation,* and the *sword of the Spirit,* which is the word of God, *praying at all times in the Spirit,* with all prayer and supplication. (Eph. 6:11–18)[13]

Other teachers have written at length about the armor of God. I won't try to match their work, but I do want to take a look at the armor in practical terms. To me, the armor of God is Paul's illustrative way of explaining how God outfits Christians for everyday life—or, in other words, how He equips His soldiers for war.

I believe the helmet of salvation means that our minds are protected with the truth of the gospel—the truth that not only is God real, but also that He lovingly sent His one and only Son to die for the sins of the world. The helmet protects our identities in Christ and keeps our minds tightly knitted to the Master's.

I think the breastplate of righteousness simply means that our hearts and vital parts are shielded from attack because the Holy Spirit is within us, churning out righteousness. The more we align with His ways, the safer we are. When the Lord shields us, our passions, emotions, and desires are free to align with the Master's heart.

I see the belt of truth as wisdom that comes from God to "hold up" and keep intact our reputations and integrity. Wisdom protects us from the embarrassment of losing our drawers in a fight by enabling us to discern right from wrong, good from bad. God's truth renews our minds every day.

I view the shoes of readiness as a metaphor for having a renewed, trained mind ready to engage in discussions of faith and share the gospel anytime, anywhere.

Brilliant scholars have pointed out that the armor provides little protection in the back. That seems to be because the territory of our hearts and minds has already been won, and we are now securely upon it, beating back the Enemy. Either we are defending a won position, or we are advancing to gain new ground. There is no need for, nor honor in, retreat.

The remaining elements of the armor—shield, sword, and prayer—seem different. Those are not strapped to the body but have to be picked up, chosen, selected. God places the main parts of the armor on us at conversion, but whether we wield the shield, sword, and prayer is up to us.

The shield is faith. In God's mercy and grace, He holds the shield over our heads for us when we are new believers, but as we grow, He shows us how to lift it ourselves. Faith is believing what we internally know to be true but cannot yet see manifest before us. In other words, when we are under spiritual attack and we hunker down beneath the truth of what God has told us, refusing to listen to the lies of the Enemy, we are using the shield of faith. We cling to the words of our Lord, letting them protect our minds from Satan's deceit. We stay there until the coast is clear and the fiery arrows of the Devil stop falling.

After the defensive shield come the offensive weapons. It is not until we can stand on our own, aware of the war and confident in our identities, that we begin to swing the sword and take the offense. The sword represents not only the Bible but every element of apprenticeship with Jesus Christ, who is the Word incarnate. When Jesus is revealed, the demons flee. When the light is turned on, the darkness dissipates. When we read Scripture and allow Jesus to lead us into a new way of living, our minds are refreshed and secured. They provide us the stability to begin to demolish the strongholds of the Devil around us by bringing truth into every situation.

The sword is a valuable tool, yet too many of us see it as the only true offensive weapon. But prayer is just as powerful. If Scripture is a sword, then prayer is a javelin. One is used in close-contact fighting, and the other can be thrown from a distance. We are told time and again to resist the Enemy in prayer[14] and that there is mighty power in the name of Jesus Christ of Nazareth.[15] This means that when we pray knowing who He is, who we are, and the authority and power He has given us, we confidently launch an assault against the influence of darkness. We pray for the freedom of our friends. We ask the Holy Spirit to give us breakthrough in addiction. We petition the Father to cancel all assignments the Enemy has against us. Prayer allows us to access the inheritance in heaven that Jesus gave to us. It allows us to command that evil bow its knee to our King Jesus.

Additional Practical Warfare Strategies

We need to seek community, relationships, and support systems. God created us for community. We are relational beings made in the image of a relational God. This means that parts of our designed lives operate best in a corporate (communal) environment. Simply put, we do best when around other people. Our spiritual gifts operate there, healthy tribal peer pressure comes into effect, encouragement runs high, and the shared wisdom is rich.

Satan's schemes work far better if they are a sneaky surprise. Once they are exposed, they lose a good portion of their power. Therefore, if we are able to talk things out with good, healthy, and wise friends, the Devil's schemes will likely be outed, and God will give someone in the group a nugget of wisdom that exposes the trap. The more we surround ourselves with objective Christian men and women who are excellent sounding boards, the more we'll avoid Satan's schemes.

I have relied on this strategy firsthand when dealing with fear. In my first book, *How to Live in Fear: Mastering the Art of Freaking Out*, I talk about my struggle with panic attacks due to panic disorder. Panic attacks thrive on the irrational. Rarely do my panic attacks make sense to anyone else but me. When my mind is telling me lies, I need anchored friends and family to remind me of reality. I need to be reminded of God's truth through those who are seeing the world rightly.

We must lock down our weak areas. Satan is an opportunist. He knows where we are weakest, and he will strike there most often. This is why Ephesians 4:27 says, "Give no opportunity to the devil." The New International Version says, "Do not give the devil a foothold." Satan is always looking for an edge, a loose place to get a grip, a chink in our armor. He will take what we give him and run with it. To combat that, we need to periodically walk through some of the following questions:

- When do I tend to fall into sin?
- How did I get deceived last time?
- What are my strengths and my weaknesses?
- Does my identity match what God says it is?
- If I were Satan, where would I strike?
- What patterns do I see emerging in my life?
- What lies do I crave to believe?

Once we know where Satan has an advantage, we can close it off—like shutting and locking the window in the back of the house to keep out thieves. This involves setting new habits that lead us away from sin, like refusing to let our minds drift into unhealthy fantasy or entering a time of fasting to break strongholds. Once we know our strengths and weaknesses, we lean into our strengths and shore up our weaknesses. For example, if you are excellent at praying for others, you can intercede wholeheartedly. If you're weak at sharing your faith because you're afraid of what other people think, you can get training to strengthen your confidence.

We need to remember that everyone gets attacked. Encountering spiritual warfare with the Devil may mean you are either a valuable target or a legitimate threat. Instead of being surprised, consider yourself warned. Each attack is a notification of future attacks.

If all of us are being assaulted, we may find it helpful to read about other peoples' experiences. Sometimes taking the time to read biographies of past saints gives us an insight into our own life patterns. As much as we like to think of ourselves as unique, we are not. Paul the apostle wrote, "No temptation has overtaken you that is not common to man" (1 Cor. 10:13). Maybe my experience resisting temptation (and sometimes succumbing to it) can help you learn to make better choices, and maybe your experience can help me.

The Devil wants to steal our identities, and he will use any form of deception to win the day. Nevertheless, we also must remember that greater is He that is in us than he that is in the world.[16] We don't have to fear. Yet some things we do make temptation more difficult to resist, while other things make it easier. God has given us everything we need for life and godliness,[17] but we need to use it well.

We need to fix our vulnerable places. Open wounds are ripe for infection. In the same way, a distorted or damaged identity invites spiritual attack and makes it harder to resist temptation. The less healthy we are, the harder life is. It's our responsibility to seek the help we need to get our lives in order. If we have trauma, we need to allow someone to help us heal. If we have baggage from our pasts, we need to let the Holy Spirit sort it and throw out what we no longer need. If we have corrupted cravings, we need to purify them through counsel and the renewal of the Word of God. If we recognize distorted thought patterns, we need to focus on God's truth to get them straightened out. So much of the difficulty in our lives comes from either unhealed hurts or self-imposed drama. Both of those create a field day for Satan's strategies. Even simple patterns of bad decisions and foolish choices can be a stew for temptation.[18] We cannot play with fire and not expect to get burned.

We need to train wiser instead of simply trying harder. If we can't resist Satan now, we must train so we can do it later. Too many of us think that we simply need to reactively dig in and fight for holiness at the moment of temptation, when, in fact, Jesus taught a lifestyle of training day by day, setting habits in motion that will pay off in the long run. His life was filled with prayer and other spiritual disciplines that strengthened Him, such as meditating on the Word of God, finding rest, seeking community, and the like. Resisting temptation is less about trying harder in the moment and more about training ahead of time. By the time the temptation starts, the skills that you were supposed to put together in practice can be put on display.

Training for temptation means teaching our bodies how to say no and denying ourselves what we crave. It's about bringing our passions under control and harnessing our drives. Practically, this means setting daily time to connect with God in prayer and reading His Word. It means slowing down our lives and making time to reflect on what God is teaching us in the moment. It means listening more than we talk or withdrawing from people for a time so that we can come back and truly be present with them. We will talk more about these types of spiritual disciplines later in the book.

We need to spend time in preventive prayer, which is one of the greatest weapons God gave us to fight temptation. Unfortunately, too many of us use prayer only in the midst of a temptation or to ask forgiveness after it's over. But the Bible speaks a lot about praying against temptation *before* it starts. For example, when Jesus became aware that Satan had asked to take Peter through severe temptation ("sifting"), the Lord's comment to Peter was, "I have prayed for you" (Luke 22:32). When Cain started to drift morally, God warned him ahead of time that sin was "crouching at the door"

(Gen. 4:7) in an attempt to get him to prepare for the attack. Even the most famous prayer in the Bible, the Lord's Prayer, says, "Lead us not into temptation, but deliver us from evil" (Matt. 6:7–13).[19] It's a preemptive prayer.

Repair is ten times harder than prevention. Doctors will tell you to take medication before the pain gets bad because you don't want to "chase the pain." The point is to wisely anticipate what's going to happen and prepare for it. That's why the Bible continually tells us to be alert.[20] We can look for predictable patterns of temptation in our lives and prepare for them. It's silly to merely hope that *this* time will be different—that's magical thinking, not wise stewardship.

We must be ruthlessly honest about what is going to happen. If you always become tempted at work by the new, beautiful co-worker, pray about that and make adjustments. Don't pursue extra time with her, take late-night meetings, or have inappropriate con-versations—or let thoughts of them consume your mind. If you always struggle with drinking too much on Wednesday nights when everyone else goes to bed, pray about it ahead of time and perhaps ask a trusted Christian friend to check in with you on Wednesdays. If you know that going to the mall stirs up your body image problems, pray and prep your spirit for the trip. Temptations don't always need to surprise us; in fact, we should see most of them coming.

But sometimes even if we see them coming, we simply aren't going to make it out unscarred.

Don't Resist; Just Run

Some temptations are too tough to make it through unharmed, and thinking that you are stronger than you really are is a recipe for disaster. Although I don't believe avoidance is more holy, I do believe it can be more effective. You need to know when it's time not to negotiate but to flee.

The story about running from temptation that's been used at every men's retreat since the dawn of time involves Joseph and Potiphar's wife, as told in Genesis 39. It goes like this: Joseph was a young stud. He was anointed, blessed, handsome, and godly. His boss, Potiphar, who was Pharaoh's captain of the guard, had a wife. She was *not* awesome. Although she could have had any other man in the kingdom, she wanted what she couldn't have: Joseph. She tried really hard to get him into bed, but it didn't work. She finally tried an all-out assault by grabbing him and demanding that he lie with her. Instead of arguing, debating, or reasoning, he ran, leaving his cloak behind in her hands.

There are some temptations you aren't going to win. The wise know when to resist and when to run. When in doubt, get out of there—fast. Too often we play around with temptation, believing we are in control of the situation. We rarely are. Thinking that we are smarter than the Enemy is prideful and stupid.

The Bible says that pride sets us up for failure.[21] The minute we think we are above temptation, we are done. Satan will use our pride every time to lure us into a problem area, because when we think we are above it, we stop being alert. Pride goes before the fall.

When Radical Steps Are Called For

Sometimes we have to take such hard-core or radical steps to escape temptation that our actions seem like overkill. Yet it's better to take radical steps up front than lose everything in the end. Jesus didn't take sin lightly, and He didn't play around with temptation. Consider His words in the gospel of Matthew:

> Woe to the world for temptations to sin! For it is necessary that temptations come, but woe to the one by whom the temptation comes! *And if your hand or your foot causes you to sin, cut it*

off and throw it away. It is better for you to enter life crippled or lame than with two hands or two feet to be thrown into the eternal fire. *And if your eye causes you to sin, tear it out and throw it away.* It is better for you to enter life with one eye than with two eyes to be thrown into the hell of fire. (Matt. 18:7–9)

No one thinks that Jesus was actually encouraging self-dismemberment, but He was using exaggeration to make a serious point. Sin isn't a game. We aren't supposed to take it lightly. It's like playing with a five-hundred-pound tiger or swimming with alligators. It's better not to. If we need to make radical decisions to avoid life-altering failures, then so be it. It's better to limp away with your pride humbled than to lose your life.

Maybe you need to transfer to another department at work because you've already consistently crossed the line with a coworker. Maybe you need to leave your laptop at work because pornography is too great of a temptation. Maybe you can't drive home via Main Street because the bar calls to you every time. Maybe you need to get off Facebook because your envy has made you bitter. Maybe you can't buy fashion magazines anymore because you are consumed with distorted body images. Maybe you need to break off certain friendships because their influence is too strong and too unhealthy. I know these things seem extreme and embarrassing, but for some they are necessary steps to take.

The Bottom Line

Temptation isn't new, and neither are Satan's schemes. Yet we're deceived by them all the time. Isn't it time to stand our ground? Pop culture has taught us that resistance is futile, but when it comes to resisting the Devil and defending our minds, resistance is not only possible but necessary.

Chapter 6

Making Monsters

Bob's Monster

Bob was lonely and wanted a companion.

He went down to the pet store and picked up a cute, little, fuzzy *wampet* (pronounced "wom-pet"). Never heard of a wampet? Imagine that a guinea pig had a baby with a Sasquatch. It looks like that.

The store clerk warned Bob that although wampets were wonderful companions and incredible snugglers, they were rather impish and untrustworthy. The key, he said, was to keep them in a cage and make sure not to overfeed them. When fed too much, they grew far faster than you could imagine, and then they were hard to contain. It sounded similar to the 1984 movie *Gremlins,* and Bob had seen that enough times that he felt he knew what to do. He took his wampet home in a special cage, along with special food and an instruction booklet.

Bob loved his new wampet. It warmed his heart to watch it wobble around in its little puffball way, and he liked when it nuzzled him and fell asleep in his lap. Bob wasn't lonely anymore. When he got home, he would lift the wampet out of the cage and playfully roll around on the floor with it. He even taught it a few tricks. Within a few days, Bob didn't hang out with friends anymore and stopped all his other activities, like his bowling league, because the wampet was such fun to play with. Despite the store clerk's warning, Bob stopped putting the wampet into the cage at all and even let it sleep with him on the bed.

The only problem was the biting.

The wampet had a temper. As long as Bob did what it wanted, it was calm, serene, and loving. If he did anything it didn't like, or if it simply got in a bad mood, it would snap at him.

And it had a huge appetite.

At first Bob fed it the food from the pet store, but he quickly realized that the wampet didn't like it and would throw a fit. It would finally wolf it down, but the process was exhausting. Eventually, Bob just fed it table scraps, and everything seemed fine. But, just as the clerk said, the wampet grew bigger every day. Unfortunately, the people food made it grow three times as fast as Bob had anticipated.

One day, when Bob came home from the office, he found the wampet had tripled in size. It was big enough to get into the cabinets, and it had consumed most of the pantry. When Bob blew up and started to yell, it rose up on its hind legs and snarled. Clearly, it was in no mood for Bob's correction, so Bob decided to deal with it later. After all, if its bites hurt when it was a baby, it could leave a significant mark now.

But that day, things changed. Bob saw that the wampet's attitude had shifted. It wasn't as fun anymore, it was far more demanding, and now that it was larger, it was getting more difficult to contain. It didn't even fit in its cage anymore. Bob decided that tomorrow he was going to put his foot down and get this critter under control. He also realized he was lonely again, so he decided to shift his focus back to his friends and maybe even start to date.

The next morning, as the wampet slept in the dark, taking up most of the bed, Bob locked all the cabinets, shut all the doors, chained the refrigerator, and walked out the door to work. On the way, he called his buddies, scheduled bowling for that night, and felt brave enough to ask Annette from sales to come over for dinner on Friday. He would make his famous Stromboli. He made a mental note to pick up some wine on the way home.

At a quarter to ten that evening, he pulled up in the driveway and unlocked the front door. The place was trashed. Furniture was overturned, the flat-screen TV was facedown, pictures were broken, and plants were shredded. Bob didn't bother to call the police. He knew who had done it. The wampet lay in a heap in the corner of the kitchen, sound asleep. It was huge. Whatever it had eaten in the pantry the night before had accelerated its growth beyond belief.

Bob went upstairs.

The next morning, Bob came out of his room and stepped around the wampet lying at the threshold. He went downstairs and surveyed the damage. He quickly figured out that he couldn't invite Annette over with the house in this condition and the wampet acting the way it was. Not only was the house a mess, but it was unsafe. On the way to work, Bob called Annette and suggested they go out to dinner that night. She thought it was odd but quickly agreed; after all, Bob was the only man at work without a comb-over.

The date went fine, but Bob couldn't stop thinking about what damage the wampet was doing back home. He was distracted enough that Annette asked him three times what was wrong. He made excuses and tried to reengage. But when it was time for him to drop her off, he didn't even walk her to the door. He had to get home to find out what terrible events had occurred. He waved to the stranded Annette and drove away.

Just as he thought, the house was destroyed. Although the wampet was slightly smaller, its viciousness had increased. After a long bout of its snarling and drooling, plus his yelling and raging, they both eventually fell asleep. Bob comforted himself with the thought that he would return the wampet to the pet store the next day.

In the morning, Bob wrestled a muzzle and leash on the wampet and forced it in the back of his Subaru Outback. It was hard to focus on driving with the wampet slamming into the gate that enclosed the rear portion of the car. Bob came screeching into the parking lot of the pet store, threw open his door, and started to march to the entrance.

But the store was closed—and not just for the day. It was closed for business entirely. There was no returning the wampet; it was Bob's to deal with forever.

He couldn't sell it. He couldn't even give it away. As he sat defeated on the curb in his disheveled clothes, the wampet wailing away in the car, he wished he had never bought a wampet at all.

Obviously, I'm speaking through parable. Giving in to our cravings can initially feel as soothing and fun as interacting with a cute baby wampet. But when we succumb to temptation over and over, it begins to grow until, eventually, it becomes a huge, scary addiction that dominates our lives.

When Temptation Crosses Over to Sin

We've spent the last few chapters looking at temptation and how to fight it. We talked about how resisting temptation strengthens our faith and character, reminds us of who we are as victors in Christ, and straightens out our distorted thoughts. But now we'll look at another reason to resist: because giving in to temptation can lead to some pretty awful places.

When fed by our bad choices, temptation grows into something far worse. It begins with an attractive or innocent-looking possibility, but if it's not removed or at least controlled, it can end up ruining our lives. Most temptations don't automatically transition to addiction, but no addict plans to be an addict. It happens when one choice leads to another and then to another. What begins with temptation crosses over into sin when it's embraced and acted upon. The Bible describes the pathway like this: "Each person is tempted when he is lured and enticed by his own desire. Then *desire when it has conceived gives birth to sin, and sin when it is fully grown brings forth death*" (James 1:14–15).

Where is the line when temptation becomes sin? Isn't that what we all want to know? The better question for us to ask is: What's at stake, and why do we need to stop the temptations before they take root? Or, perhaps, what happens if I cross the line and want to get back?

All of us have taken temptation too far already—not just once but thousands of times. The only reason that most of us didn't receive the full consequences of our choices is the mercy and grace of God. If God didn't step in, all temptation would result in our deaths (emotionally, mentally, spiritually, or physically). Praise the Lord that He is with us and that the Holy Spirit is helping us navigate all of this!

Acting on temptation is sin. What if we made a habit of sinning? What if we started doing something that was excessively difficult to stop? Where would that lead?

Compulsion

Our first stop on the slippery slope toward addiction is compulsion. Compulsion is the intense desire to do something even when we know it's best not to. The difference between addiction and compulsion is how much we are willing to pay for the thing we want. The object of our compulsion is not necessarily something bad or negative; the negative part is the loss of control.

I'm sure we can all relate to intense cravings somewhere in our lives. It could be the hankering for dessert that we know we shouldn't eat after a full meal. It could be the "retail therapy" we practice to make ourselves feel better. It could be spending countless hours on the computer, avoiding any human interaction. Compulsion is not only about making a bad decision but also about the intense feeling that we *have to* make a bad decision. It's when something internally compels us.

Could we stop? Sure, but do we? No. And therein lies the problem: we justify the compulsion because we know that if worse came to worst, we *could* stop—so we keep going.

I have never had an addiction. But I can assure you that not only have I been tempted daily (and fallen), but also I've fought compulsions far more times than I would like to admit. Some have been so intense that I questioned whether I was crossing over into addiction. We will talk about addiction in the next chapter, but I want to take a full chapter here to talk about compulsion because I think that most of humanity—including the church—battles it.

I refer to the pathway from temptation to addiction as a slippery slope because we may intend to slide to one place—and even make an agreement with sin to get there—but we'll always slip farther than we intended. We want to "walk on the wild side"; we don't want the wild side to follow us home. We want to live dangerously, but we don't want the consequences. We want to flirt but not follow through. We want the rest of the cake, but we don't want the weight gain. We want the attention; we don't want the stalker. We dip our emotions in a polluted pool to get a drink, and we never stop wanting more. When the lure for more is overly compelling, we are experiencing compulsion.

The scary thing is that we don't know how hard it will be to stop until we actually try.

Compulsion causes us to spend too much on whatever the temptation is. Even when we clear our heads and realize that we made a bad decision, the craving rises up, and we do it again. Even when there are significant consequences, we don't want to stop. Whatever we're craving becomes the most important thing. Even if others plead with us to stop, we find a way to carry on.

Making Monsters

Our cravings are like Bob's wampet: what we feed grows.

The difference between interest, temptation, desire, compulsion, and addiction is the size of the monster. When it's tiny, cute, and fuzzy, it's *interest* and possibly *temptation*. When it grows to the size of a dog and makes a mess, it's probably *desire*. When it's bigger than we are and dealing with it becomes a battle, it's *compulsion*. When it runs us out of our own house, it's *addiction*.

We are all making monsters.

When we say yes one time to a bad choice, it's easier to say yes the next time. When we cave to temptation, it's harder to say no when it comes again. When we sin, the Devil gets a foothold. The more we feed the flesh, the stronger it becomes in our lives. At some point, it grows beyond our ability to control it and causes damage. When it pushes us around and dictates decisions, compulsion is firmly rooted. The Bible would call it the beginning of bondage.

Mental Slavery

Slavery is "submission to a dominating influence."[1] Slavery can be physical, but it can also be mental, emotional, and spiritual. For the Christian, bondage to sin is a critical concern. That is why the apostle Paul wrote,

> *Let not sin therefore reign in your mortal body, to make you obey its passions.* . . . Do you not know that *if you present yourselves to anyone as obedient slaves, you are slaves of the one whom you obey, either of sin,* which leads to death, or of obedience, which leads to righteousness? . . . For just as *you once presented your members as slaves to impurity and to lawlessness leading to more lawlessness,* so now present your members as slaves to righteousness leading to sanctification. (Rom 6:12, 16, 19)

We have a choice: Will we be enslaved by obedience to God, which, ironically, is a slavery that sets us free, or will we be enslaved to sin, which pulls us away from our true identities as God's children? One choice leads to a cleaner mind, a purer heart, and looking more like Jesus. The other leads to confusion, dysfunction, distortion, and more sin.

It is possible to make so many bad decisions and create such bad habits that we are no longer able to make good decisions freely. As Christians we are called by God to live as He would, to please His heart, and to honor Him, but that becomes extremely difficult if we have allowed our sin nature to dominate us. Not only are we dishonoring our Lord, but if we continue in sinful behaviors, we run the risk of completely losing our God-designed selves.

Jesus died to set us free. He broke the chains, He finished the job on the cross, and He made it possible for us not to be in bondage to sin. He turned us from slaves of sin to victors over sin. He showed us the path to finding the real us that He created us to be. Yet we still forget who we are. Instead of living freely, we have stumbled into, chosen, returned to, and submitted to slavery once again—this time chaining ourselves willingly.

What is wrong with us?

Sin is enticing and dangerous. And the more we taste, the more we want. Unfortunately, too often we are willing to trade our freedom for it. If we truly knew what we were getting into, we would run the other way. Part of mastering our minds is thinking right thoughts, coming to the right conclusions, and making the right choices. How can we do that if we keep getting bombarded by compulsions that push us this way and that? How are we supposed to keep our thoughts in check if hidden land mines are planted all around us? Too many times, we suddenly find that a few decisions have put us in a bad place and we don't know the way back home. What we thought was going to be a little "me time" led us into emotional captivity.

Why don't we see it coming? Where are the warnings? If there's a massive cliff up ahead where we could fall to our deaths, don't you think there should be a sign telling us not to get too close?

Oh, there are plenty of signs. We just ignore them, remove them, or paint over them.

The Conscience: A Moral Road Sign

In 1940, Disney released its second theatrical film, *Pinocchio*, based on the story written by Carlo Collodi of Italy and originally titled *Storie di un Burattino*, "The Story of a Marionette."

A famous scene in the movie between the Blue Fairy, Pinocchio, and Jiminy Cricket goes like this:

The Blue Fairy: [to Pinocchio] You must learn to choose
between right and wrong.
Pinocchio: Right and wrong? But how will I know?
Jiminy Cricket: [watching] How'll he know!
The Blue Fairy: [to Pinocchio] Your conscience will tell you.

Pinocchio: What's a conscience?

Jiminy Cricket: What's a conscience! I'll tell ya! A conscience is that still small voice that people won't listen to. That's just the trouble with the world today . . .

Pinocchio: Are you my conscience?

Jiminy Cricket: Who, me?

The Blue Fairy: Would you like to be Pinocchio's conscience?

Jiminy Cricket: [blushing] Well, uh, I . . . Uh-huh [nodding].[2]

Your conscience is the little voice inside your heart that tells you what to do. It's the cautious voice, the moral voice, the thoughts that warn you when you are ready to step over a line. It might sound like your mother or your spouse. It's the restraining voice, and it carries all the trappings of the voice of wisdom.

Just following the scene above, Jiminy sings a sweet little song that repeats the words of the Blue Fairy to "always let your conscience be your guide." Yet, as much as I respect Jiminy for his clothing style, I cannot agree with his wisdom for life. His advice sounds good, but it's faulty. You see, our consciences are self-set, and they're only as accurate and helpful as we make them.[3] It would be wonderful if our consciences were a direct download from God that truly measured right and wrong, but they simply aren't.[4] Our consciences are tailored by our beliefs, thoughts, decisions, and actions. That makes them highly suspect and significantly unreliable. Just because we don't *feel* guilty doesn't mean we aren't.

That is why the apostle Paul wrote, "My conscience is clear, but that does not make me innocent" (1 Cor. 4:4 NIV).[5]

If our minds are healthy and connected to the Lord, then our consciences will be more aligned to the Master's Mind. If our consciences are ruled by worldly thoughts, our alarms may not be set right. The goal should be to follow the voice of the Holy Spirit, not simply our own moral codes. But if our consciences are set to an earthly standard, they will justify our hearts, minds, and choices. Alignment is everything.

However, if our consciences are properly set and trained, we can use them to our advantage. A conscience can be a wonderful tool for righteous and wise living,[6] but we have a lot of work to do. All of us could use an inner guard and guide. How amazing would it be if we always knew what was right and wrong, good and bad, wise and foolish, moral and immoral? Then we could recognize clearly that we knew what was right but chose differently. We could feel confident that we would know the pathway back to integrity. We would be fully informed. But we cannot get out what we do not put in. If there is no truth in the framework, the results are going to be foolishness.

Shaping and Using Our Consciences Rightly

A conscience is like a computer program. It gathers data and reports what it sees, making decisions based on the parameters it was given. This makes it unique to each person. One person's conscience may be set to social norms so that when he burps loudly at a dinner party, he says, "Excuse me." Another person's conscience may be highly tuned to religious matters so that everything seems like a sin and guilt is a daily emotion. Another's may be formed solely by her parents, and alarms go off when she does something that doesn't match their values. We're influenced by our backgrounds and by those around us. The only way to be able to trust the accuracy of our consciences is to rebuild them from the ground up according to the Master's Mind.

The Bible explains that we are able to shape our consciences and bring them into alignment with the heart of God.[7] This involves pouring in His truth and His mind-set and submitting our version of truth to His.

The author of Hebrews used a powerful illustration for his Jewish brothers regarding this concept. He explained that because Jesus took care of our sin and made us righteous before God, we can draw close to the heart of God without fear of being rejected. As we get closer to Him, our minds, hearts, and consciences are purified, cleansed from the garbage of this world, and linked more tightly with His method of thinking and the identity He wants for His children.

> Therefore, brothers, since we have confidence to enter the holy places by the blood of Jesus, by the new and living way that he opened for us through the curtain, that is, through his flesh, and since we have a great priest over the house of God, *let us draw near with a true heart in full assurance of faith, with our hearts sprinkled clean from an evil conscience and our bodies washed with pure water.* (Heb. 10:19–22)

Eventually, as our minds are renewed, our consciences are dialed in. Practically speaking, this is done through reading the Word of God, listening to accurate messages from godly teachers, studying the Bible individually or in a group, getting wise counsel, and spending significant time in prayer. God allowed the authors of the Bible to highlight the importance of wisdom over and over. The more we seek godly wisdom, the more accurate our consciences will become.

As our consciences are appropriately refashioned, we can begin to use them for what they were intended to be: a guide. A conscience is supposed to be an alarm that sounds when we step out of line. Yet it can also be a soothing voice that assures us we are on the right path. A conscience is notoriously unstable and untrustworthy, but we can get to a place where it reveals what God deems to be true and what the Holy Spirit speaks to our hearts. Therefore, if we are able to align our actions with our fully, wisely formed consciences, we travel far closer to living the way God intends.[8]

Slaying Our Monsters

What you feed grows; what you starve shrinks.

When our cravings are out of control and we are compulsively heading toward addiction, we still have time to rid ourselves of our monsters. It's a lot of work, and we certainly will wish we'd never given in to temptation in the first place, but it's possible. The only reason Bob kept his wampet was that he had no one to tell him how to get rid of it properly.

It's tempting to keep the monsters in our lives as long as we reduce them to a manageable level, and that is what both the sinful parts of us and the Devil want us to do. We fantasize about how wonderful it would be to shrink the temptation down to a place where we can control it and use it as we please. *We don't have to get rid of it*, we think. *We can simply contain it.* But some monsters shouldn't be contained. Some monsters should never be owned at all.

I have to admit that I, too, have fallen prey to the "let's just shrink that back down to a manageable level" ploy. The truth is, we need to get these monsters out of our lives once and for all before they cause some real damage. We want actual transformation that sets us free, not simply alleged change that can be quickly undone. So how do we shrink these monsters and root them out?

It's no surprise that God knows how to remove monsters better than we do. He hates them, and they hate Him. Therefore, if we are going to get rid of any monsters, we begin by asking God to enter into the situation and help us take back control of our minds. Everything powerful begins with prayer.

We can invite God in only when we admit our powerlessness to bring true and deep change to our lives. Only God knows what is wrong and what must be altered. Only God knows what He built us to be and what we can fully become. When we ask Him to have His way in our lives, we must match that with a determination to follow His direction. We can no longer lean on our own understanding, but in all our ways we must acknowledge Him, and He will direct our paths.[9] Instead, we have to start making good decisions, based on biblical principles. We start acting in a loving fashion toward ourselves and toward others. We follow through on the restoration of healthy relationships, and we reestablish a support system. We submit to wise, mature, and godly guidance. We seek out professionals in the areas of our struggles.

Respect the Process

I am a pastor who has done a lot of counseling in my decades of ministry. I have seen and heard pretty much every struggle known to man. Nothing surprises me anymore. I have walked through both heartbreaking tragedy and spine-tingling victory. I have seen hundreds struggle with addictions and thousands wrestle with compulsion. Yet, only a handful of all of those I've seen with behavioral compulsions and addictions have experienced miraculous healing and instantaneous removal of symptoms, habits, and temptations. Almost every person I've worked with has had to walk out his or her freedom hand in hand with the Lord, day by day.

I think the Lord does that on purpose.

I'm not sure the church appreciates process. We want all of our problems, difficulties, and troubles to simply go away. We think that God set up a system whereby if we love Him enough, everything will be resolved instantly. But God doesn't work that way. If we walked into the bondage through a hundred choices, He walks us out through a hundred choices. Why not just heal us and take away our cravings overnight? Because we might not own the healing or respect the process, and that would leave us vulnerable to future slavery. God is in the business of permanent deliverance, not temporary rescue.

Healing and restoring behavioral issues takes time and effort. It's tough to uproot stubborn habits and deny self. It's difficult to have to make a determined decision that defies desire every day. It's no fun to grit our teeth when our flesh screams out for feeding. Although prayer is crucial and a significant part of the healing, talking to God doesn't make things disappear as quickly as we wish it would. Reading the Bible doesn't remove physiological nicotine cravings. Going to church doesn't automatically stop lust and porn addiction. There's a process.

In this process, guilt and shame are less healthy emotions than honesty and hope. We are going to fail along the way, yet failure must not destroy us. Our identities are not based on our performances but on who God says we are and who He is making us to be. We must allow ourselves to walk like humans, fail like humans, and be restored as humans. The process of becoming healthy can be difficult and long. Please don't give up. The reward is a life of freedom and victory.

We are complicated beings made up of emotions, physical components, mental processes, spiritual layers, and relational dynamics. Compulsion tends to infiltrate all these elements, and, therefore, the Lord must lead us through healing in each area in a way that allows us to gain control and renew our minds. If we train our bodies to crave a dopamine rush in our brains, we need to retrain them to function without it. If we establish dysfunctional relationship patterns, we need to reestablish healthy patterns. If we cope improperly with the effects of abuse, a counselor needs to help us mentally reframe our lives. It's not as simple as just being a better Christian.

Don't get me wrong: church is an incredibly helpful tool, the Bible realigns our worldview like nothing else, and prayer is our lifeline. I'm merely pointing out that there are many aspects to how God designed us, and He has given us tools to address each affected layer. We need to use the right tools for the right problems, always centering God's role in the process.

Chapter 7

Hostile Takeover

If we continue to ignore God's help and give way to our compulsions, we can find ourselves stuck in thought patterns that we neither want nor enjoy. We lose control of our minds—literally. It's as though hostile forces have taken over.

In this chapter I'll focus on the most common mental and emotional takeovers I've observed—what I call the Five Horsemen of the Mental Apocalypse, or the Big Five: depression, anxiety, anger, idolatry, and addiction. Just being human makes us susceptible to all five, but some of us are fully dominated by them.

I am neither an addiction specialist, nor a psychiatrist, nor a clinical therapist. But I am a pastor who has counseled countless people with mental illness. Although I have personally lived some of the terrible things we are going to talk about, and I've certainly seen my fair share of friends lost in addiction, I'm not going to pretend that this is my specialty. I will leave that to the professionals. My goal is to talk about this subject at a thirty-thousand-foot, theoretical level and touch on some practical tools that have brought freedom to me and those I love.

The main question in my mind is this: What do we do when

negative behaviors and thoughts take hold to such a degree that we are no longer calling the shots on our decisions?

Almost any craving can fully dominate someone if given the right environment in which to grow out of control.

It may feel dishonoring to say that praying and trying really hard won't cause God to lift us out of bondage. Maybe it's simply too scary to believe we can go down a dark road and not be able to find our way back. Even modern-day secular America, which still believes in the "pull-yourself-up-by-your-bootstraps" theory, refuses to accept that it's possible to be in a place where you can't think your way into a better future. But it's true.

Sometimes we are born into it: crack babies born hooked on drugs, children raised in dysfunctional environments, people with genetic proclivities or extreme addictive personalities. And, of course, we're all born into original sin.

Sometimes we walk ourselves into it: smoking, drinking, drugs, sex and porn, hoarding, and other addictions.

And sometimes God hands us over to it.

When the Mighty Fall

History speaks of one of the greatest kings this world has ever known: Nebuchadnezzar II of Babylon. Born around 632 BC as a prince under his father, Nabopolassar, the pioneer of the Chaldean Empire, Nebuchadnezzar found himself a military leader by his early twenties and took the throne five years later after his father's death. He reigned for an impressive forty-three years.

Following in the footsteps of his father, who defeated the Assyrian Empire and took control of Babylon, Nebuchadnezzar made a name for himself as a warrior king. He won the famous battle of Carchemish against the Egyptians the year he was called to the throne. He fused his alliance with the Medes by marriage and expanded his territory by military force until he controlled much of the Middle East and all the trade routes across Mesopotamia.

Perhaps his most famous military exploit began with his conquering the area of Palestine on March 16, 597 BC. Eleven years later, to quell a Jewish rebellion, he led an eighteen-month siege to take Jerusalem. He destroyed the famous temple of Solomon and exiled tens of thousands of Jews from their homeland.

His fame wasn't simply military. Nebuchadnezzar was known the world over for his reconstruction of Babylon—expanding more than five hundred acres—and other extraordinary building projects. He is given credit for one of the Seven Wonders of the World—the hanging gardens of Babylon—and his Ishtar Gate of the city is legendary. He was so impressive that Saddam Hussein sought to claim his reincarnated personality. Hussein named one of his guard divisions after the ancient king and began rebuilding ancient Babylon in his honor, inscribing on the bricks, "To King Nebuchadnezzar in the reign of Saddam Hussein."

But I am most interested in the biblical accounts of this king. Nebuchadnezzar is mentioned in at least nine books of the Old Testament and is featured in some of its most dramatic stories: the great gold statue dream, where God showed him the future empires of the world; and the fiery furnace incident involving Shadrach, Meshach, and Abednego, the young Jewish boys who were thrown in the fire but miraculously saved. I want to focus on a small passage in the book of Daniel, written by the young prophet who worked for this king:

> All this came upon King Nebuchadnezzar. At the end of twelve months he was walking on the roof of the royal palace of Babylon, and the king answered and said, "Is not this great Babylon, which I have built by my mighty power as a royal residence and for the glory of my majesty?" While the words were still in the king's

mouth, there fell a voice from heaven, "O King Nebuchadnezzar, to you it is spoken: *The kingdom has departed from you, and you shall be driven from among men, and your dwelling shall be with the beasts of the field. And you shall be made to eat grass like an ox, and seven periods of time shall pass over you, until you know that the Most High rules the kingdom of men and gives it to whom he will.*" Immediately the word was fulfilled against Nebuchadnezzar. He was driven from among men and ate grass like an ox, and his body was wet with the dew of heaven till his hair grew as long as eagles' feathers, and his nails were like birds' claws. *At the end of the days I, Nebuchadnezzar, lifted my eyes to heaven, and my reason returned to me*, and I blessed the Most High. . . . At the same time my reason returned to me, and for the glory of my kingdom, my majesty and splendor returned to me. . . . *Now I, Nebuchadnezzar, praise and extol and honor the King of heaven, for all his works are right and his ways are just; and those who walk in pride he is able to humble.* (Dan. 4:28–37)

This great and powerful king lost his mind. He became like an animal in what looked like a form of temporary insanity. Some scholars argue that it couldn't have happened that way, but I am certain Daniel knew exactly whom he worked for and what took place. The Lord drove Nebuchadnezzar to desperation to correct his attitude, discipline his pride and arrogance against God, and humble the self-absorbed monarch.

As He did with this prideful king, sometimes God needs to hand us over to whatever craving we have sold our soul for in order to motivate us to fight to get out. And like Nebuchadnezzar, we can lose control.

No matter how invincible we feel, no matter how disciplined a moral life we lead, we are susceptible to losing ourselves, our minds, and our holds on our identities in Christ. We can become something we never intended—animals doing things so contrary to our nature that we wonder if we are still ourselves at all. Although it may not technically be insanity, it sure feels like it.

However, unlike for Nebuchadnezzar, for most of us the "hostile takeover" is not judgment but a result of our own choices and proclivities. God leveled Nebuchadnezzar for pride and arrogance, and once that was done, He lifted His hand immediately and miraculously. That's not normally how it works. Although God does sometimes teach us about ramifications by opening the gate when we constantly press on it to get the greener grass on the other side, He is not doing so in judgment but in loving discipline. And unlike Nebuchadnezzar's experience, our pathway out of addiction and hostile takeovers isn't normally easy and instant. It's a process. Nevertheless, his story reminds us that even the mighty fall sometimes, and no mind is invulnerable.

The Five Horsemen of the Mental Apocalypse

The Big Five—depression, anxiety, anger, idolatry, and addiction—share a number of similarities. Each one can grow in its stranglehold. Each has triggers. Each is deeply seated in our brain patterns. Each needs to be dug out from the roots, not just trimmed like a branch. Each has a spiritual core but heavily involves all aspects of the human being: physical, emotional, mental, and spiritual.

Although these horsemen may have a basis in chemicals or hormones and can even be present from birth, we can exacerbate them with our own choices. What may begin as a genetic distortion can flourish into dysfunctional thinking. Therefore, they all tend to share a similar pathway of growth in intensity. For a person with a serotonin absorption problem that makes him or her more susceptible to anxiety or depression, certain choices can either increase the problem or deescalate the situation. If increased amounts of testosterone make someone prone to aggression, irritability, and anger, he or she can take measures to bring it under control. No matter what components are involved, we can always make things better through our choices and our mind-sets.

As I mentioned in the previous chapter, the difference between temptation, craving, compulsion, and addiction is the size of the monster. For example, if you really, really want to take a pharmaceutical to keep your energy up but can still deny yourself the drug, you are dealing with craving and compulsion. However, if your wife is begging you to stop taking the drug, you're lying to cover up your behavior, your attitude has changed, you're neglecting responsibilities, and you're spending a lot of money on your habit, you are squarely in addiction territory.

By the time we get to the point of "hostile takeover," we have ceded control of our minds. We no longer have the Master's Mind. And we certainly aren't able to offer our minds as acts of worship to our Master. Our thoughts are distorted; we have faulty mind-sets and cannot think clearly.

Let's turn our attention to the Five Horsemen and examine them in light of hostile mental takeovers.

Depression

Depression can be defined as a "a psychoneurotic or psychotic disorder marked especially by sadness, inactivity, difficulty in thinking and concentration, a significant increase or decrease in appetite and time spent sleeping, feelings of dejection and hopelessness, and sometimes suicidal tendencies."[1] Sometimes its symptoms can also manifest in fatigue, a complete lack of feeling, and a loss of interest in activities or hobbies. At its core, depression involves a negativity toward life.

It's entirely normal to get "down" sometimes. It's also completely understandable to feel depressed when we sustain loss, hurt, or emotional pain. The concern is when those feelings become overwhelming, won't stop, interfere with normal life, or have an impact on our physical bodies. Periodic seasons of sadness about disappointing elements of life are expected, but when depression is chronic (long term) and seems unrelated to current events, we need to take a deeper look.

Depression has many root causes, including chemical levels, hormonal levels, challenging circumstances, and learned behavior. Regardless of the cause, the solution may be elusive at best or unobtainable at worst. Some of us have to live our entire lives wrestling with depression. Thankfully, the medical field's understanding of depression has advanced significantly, and a number of effective treatments, including tailored medications, are available.

My greatest frustration with depression—as well as anxiety, which we'll cover next—is that it leads to thoughts that are contrary to God's truth. God says we are precious, we are valuable, we have a purpose, and we have a bright future with Him. Yet when we're depressed, we believe lies that crush our spirits. On a good day, we wouldn't dare think such things, but during dark nights of the soul (deep depressive episodes), we aren't thinking correctly at all and find ourselves believing the unthinkable (for example, *God doesn't love me, I have no purpose or value, I'm all alone and abandoned, I'm a failure, I may as well not exist,* and so on).

I do not believe that most bouts of depression or anxiety begin with a spiritual cause. But I certainly believe that Satan will gleefully take advantage of a prime situation. The father of lies loves nothing more than to fill our minds full of garbage when we are most vulnerable. During depression, we lack not only the strength to fight the lies but the resolve as well.

Can God miraculously and instantaneously heal depression?

Absolutely. It would be as easy for Him as curing a common cold. But does He? Not usually. Usually, we are called to steward our bodies and work with what we have been given. We need to realize that depression is serious and that we need help to navigate it.

While we pursue professional help and insight, we have choices to make about how we are going to live and where we will allow our minds to go. Even if we have diagnosed depression, we still have authority and power to shape our minds. Don't let the Enemy convince you there's no point in trying or that nothing you do will help; that's simply not true. Like most wars of our minds, it's a battle of inches. Every little bit helps incrementally. Collectively, we gain the upper hand.

A precious woman in my life who wrestles with depression gave me her personal list of depression helps and insights, which I keep in my phone:

Six Things That Make Depression Worse

1. Avoiding situations or decisions and having to carry the weight of guilt over it
2. Lack of discipline and not feeling proud of my choices
3. Sinful indulgences that distance me from God
4. Lack of a dream, hope, or something to look forward to
5. Too much self-focus
6. Chemical, physical, or circumstantial factors

Ten Things That Help Me Get Out of Depressive Episodes

1. Making a schedule—sometimes it's literally an hourly schedule. Realigning for balance. Fitting in what needs to

be fit in. Doing so stops the feeling of being overwhelmed and reminds me of my priorities.

2. Staying disciplined with chores. Doing what needs to be done.
3. Exercising.
4. Being around people more to fill my emotional bank and get me out of my own head.
5. Praying on my knees before God, literally. Getting serious about it (not halfway, lukewarm, or distracted). He will meet me there.
6. Asking trusted friends and family for prayer. This forces humility, blasts through shame, and fights the pride of pretending I have life all together.
7. Making goals. Goals are dreams, larger than day-to-day plans.
8. Staying busy. Isolation feeds into self-obsession.
9. Seeking inspiration from God. When we lack vision and hope we cry out, "Lord, inspire me."
10. Serving others—before yourself. Seeing their situations and entering their life stories.

Depression lives in our minds; therefore, the greatest victory we can have is the renewal of our thoughts. Despite the challenges of chemical or hormonal issues, we get to decide what thoughts we dwell upon. Depression doesn't get to decide that we feel worthless or that nothing matters. God gets to determine our worth and the value of our actions. As we submit our negative thoughts to Him and let Him tell us what is true through His Word and prayer, little by little we can start to think differently and begin to master our minds.

Anxiety

This subject is intensely personal for me. I have struggled with diagnosed panic disorder since I was six years old. As I mentioned previously, I wrote an entire book on this subject called *How to Live in Fear.* I have taken medication every day since 1996, and it has allowed me to live a relatively normal, productive, and successful life. Yet I also know that my worst battles of spiritual warfare have been fought against me with fear.

Too many people were raised in church to believe that if you just loved Jesus more, you wouldn't struggle with fear. None of the leaders in those churches had a diagnosed panic disorder; I can assure you of that. You see, when Jesus talked about fear, anxiety, and worry,[2] I believe He was talking about normal struggles of life—worrying about how the day will go, what will happen with our jobs, how our children will turn out, whether we really have to stand up in front of everyone and risk rejection—things like that. What He wasn't referring to was a state of perpetual fight-or-flight terror caused by the brain's inability to function properly. Yet His wisdom is true for those of us with generalized anxiety disorders and those without. We all have decisions to make about where we will let our minds go.

Whether we have diagnosed anxiety or are primarily worried about the future or what we see on the news, we have choices. What are we going to focus on? When fear rises in our lives, how easy will it be for the Enemy to derail us? Where will our minds go when circumstances get scary?

God is a God of peace. As a child, I memorized 2 Timothy 1:7 in the New King James Version, which says, "God has not given us a spirit of fear, but of power and of love and of a sound mind." It became one of my life verses. God wants His children to know the safety that comes with being His child. When the world starts to go crazy, He wants us to keep our minds fixed on Him and His love for us. When the disciples screamed at Him in fear, "Don't you care if we drown?" during the storm on the Sea of Galilee, Jesus' response was, "Why are you so afraid? Have you still no faith?" (Mark 4:40).

Although that might translate with a rude tone, it was gentle but firm. He meant, "Why is fear a thing for you? Don't you know Me? Don't you know My love and protection over you? Don't you know that I am the Master of all creation and that all things bow before My will? Don't you know that if you are Mine, then anything that wishes to touch you has to get My approval first?"

In my first book, I refer to my three greatest lifesavers when it comes to mind-numbing fear:

1. The Bible (Word of God)
2. Prayer
3. Worship[3]

The Bible gets our heads into a different frame of mind. It's harder to be afraid when you read about a God who can walk Hebrew boys through fire, shut the mouths of lions, resurrect the dead, destroy the works of the Devil, and raise Himself to life. When we see that our Master is in charge, we can change our minds to align with His, and His peace flows in. It's a matter of focusing more on the Lord's power and less on the world's problems.

Prayer matters because if anyone can do something about our situations, it's our heavenly Father. Why not invite Him into the situation you're anxious about? When I'm in a panic attack, prayer is my lifeline. I cry out to Him, knowing that He hears me, and I await His response. Many times He doesn't answer the way I want Him to—with instant relief—but He always answers with the best solution. Just as calling 911 gives us confidence that help is on the way, so too does prayer bring in the big guns: the Master of the Universe who is greater than anything facing us. Prayer helps us keep focused on who God is, reminding us that He has the power to deliver. It keeps us from feeling helpless, because we know we have turned over our situations and emotions to the Almighty One.

Worship is powerful because the Bible tells us that when we focus on God's glory and His adoration, He fights our battles for us. Like Joshua and the people of Israel walking around Jericho and praising God until the Lord tore down the walls, so too can we lock our minds into the worship and praise of our mighty God and allow Him to defeat our enemies.[4] Not only does God allow music to transport us into an emotional place of receiving from Him, but when He is praised, the Enemy is shut down.

The key to all three of these tools is our mind-sets—focusing on God and who He is rather than on our own situations and our fears.

Anger

There's probably no hostile takeover or horseman we try harder to justify than anger, rage, bitterness, hatred, and unforgiveness. After all, we wouldn't be angry if the situation didn't deserve it, right? Ephesians 4:26 tells us there is a way to be angry and not sin, but that's not the kind of anger I mean. I'm talking about living in a state of constant frustration and bitterness where we blow up for no reason. It's like an overfilled glass of water—one tiny drop causes us to spill. Sometimes we live under a perpetual cloud of doom that casts darkness into our souls.

So much of our anger stems from our identities, our inability to repair from hurt, and our need to develop healthy coping skills. We know that it affects our moods, our sleep, our dreams, our behavior, and our relationships. So what do we do? Psychologists, therapists, and counselors have developed amazing ways of dealing with anger and getting to the root causes and triggers, and there are many resources at our disposal. I do not want to minimize the deep work that may be needed to lift our hearts out of a pit of anger. However, I do want to highlight just one part of the process that seems to be vital to taking back territory that has been lost to anger, rage, hatred, and bitterness against other people: forgiveness.

I know we don't want to hear that. If there's any word that will send an angry person over the edge, it's this one. Forgiveness feels as though it violates everything about our human nature and sense of justice. We don't want to forgive. We don't want to let go of our anger and resentment.

But unforgiveness is toxic. When we hold grudges and anger toward people or situations, it eats us alive. When we are continually angry, we think that it's up to us to right any wrongs done against us. We feel we need to grab for what's rightfully ours and push back at those who get in our way. We think that we are hanging on to our anger to make them pay, and that if we forgive them then they are getting away with it. But nothing could be further from the truth. When we live in bitterness and anger, we hurt only ourselves. Our hatred doesn't hurt the one we are angry at; it's self-destructive. It's wisely been said, "Forgiveness is setting a prisoner free and realizing that prisoner is you."

Forgiving others is the smartest thing a Christian can do. When we forgive, we are not pretending that the hurt didn't happen; we are looking it straight in the face and calling it what it was: evil. But then we are handing it over to the greater Judge. We put it in the hands of the expert, the Lawgiver, the King. We aren't "letting it go" as much as we are releasing it to the authority. Then we can move on and live in the grace, love, and power of Christ. It's not on us to hold others accountable; that's God's job. It's not our responsibility to make them pay; we couldn't dole out a punishment any greater than what the Almighty can. And truly, if we think about it enough, we know we need to forgive because of all that He has forgiven us for.

Yes, what others did to us was unacceptable. Yes, it was wrong. Yes, they should have to answer for it. But that process isn't ours to mete out. Each of us is merely one sinner complaining about another sinner. If Jesus, the sinless Lamb of God, would die a sinner's death and face separation from the Father for something He never did, then how can we not release another person into the hands of a just, albeit loving and grace-filled, God?

Idolatry

Idolatry is the worship of anything other than the one true God. I could write a treatise on all the things that we worship alongside or in place of God: money, fame, sex, power, influence, pleasure, laziness, each other, superstars, athletes, prestige, intelligence, beauty, wit, charisma, and the list goes on. But when it all boils down, we are worshiping created things rather than the Creator,[5] and our favorite subject is ourselves. We love ourselves more than we love God.

In the Old Testament, God consistently rebuked Israel and the surrounding pagan nations for idolatry. Most nations He judged as "serving other gods," but when it came to His own people, His chosen and promised nation of Israel, He used a different descriptor: spiritual adultery. To God, everything hinges on relationship with Him. He does not think in terms of systems or codes; He thinks in terms of love. When we serve or worship something other than Him, we love that thing more, even while we are committed to Him. That's a wonderful definition of adultery.

Perhaps the most blatant form of idolatry today is entitlement. Mankind has been entitled since Adam and Eve; we have always believed that we deserve more and that the world should revolve around us. At the heart of all sin is the elevation of self and the removal of God from His rightful throne. At the heart of selfishness is pride that we have the right to say no to our Creator, that we are the ultimate Master instead of Him.

All sin comes down to the idolatry of self. It's not only preeminent in our culture; it's also overtaken our minds. Try to fast one day from thinking about yourself and tell me how far you get. My record is two seconds.

The solution to this crisis is to restore the proper worship of God and return to a mind-set of biblical humility. Remember the definition of humility we've been using? It's not thinking less *of* yourself but thinking less *about* yourself. Until we shift our souls from self-centered to God-centered, we will remain victims of a hostile takeover.

So much of idolatry is simply wrong thinking that begins with a faulty premise and lives in lies. Therefore, as with other hostile takeovers, much of the solution is saturating ourselves with truth. We need to see God as He really is. One of the phrases the Old Testament uses for praising God is to "magnify His name."[6] That means to make it as big as it should be. Idolatry can exist only when we think of God as small, containable, controllable, and able to be manipulated. But when we lift up and exalt God, pride and idolatry seem silly and foolish. Likewise, as we consider who we are in light of who He is—sinful mankind desperately in need of a Savior—we won't dream of telling God what to do or how to do it, much less trading Him for something of this earth.

Addiction

Instead of trying to touch on all the types of addictions, I want to focus on the most common: drugs, alcohol, nicotine, sex, and gambling.

I define *drugs* as any substance, manufactured or natural, legal or illegal, that alters our life experience.[7] Just because something is legal doesn't mean it's good for you. Just because a substance isn't physically addictive (take marijuana, for example) doesn't mean it's not emotionally or mentally addictive. *Alcohol* is by many standards the most legalized drug in America and world-wide. Just because something is socially acceptable doesn't mean it's not dangerous.[8] *Nicotine* is still an issue, even though smoking has become far less cool than it used to be.[9] But even with that paradigm shift, millions are still addicted, and more are being added daily. *Sex* is highly addictive because of what it does to our brains. It chemically alters our minds with a euphoric and numbing sensation, which is always a temptation to crave.[10] Finally, I mention *gambling* because I respect the pull that it can have and the addictive cycle it can start. I am not an antigambling man, but I do understand that gambling holds an intense attraction for some and has ruined many a life.

When addiction controls us, it's poison to our soul. The Bible says that we are not to be mastered by anything: "'All things are lawful for me,' but not all things are helpful. *'All things are lawful for me,' but I will not be dominated by anything*" (1 Cor. 6:12).[11]

Many of us hear condemnation and shame in that verse, but I hear victory. Why? Because God's calling is God's enabling. If God commands us to stop something, that means He will give us the ability to stop. A good parent never punishes a child for something he or she cannot control. God is a good Father, and, therefore, if He gives us a directive, it's possible for us. Try reading the Bible through that lens, seeing that all rules, commands, regulations, and laws are whispers of victory. It's freeing and encouraging.

God will help us, and He promises eventual victory. But if we walk into the trap of our addiction, we'll still have to struggle and work our way out.

What Addiction Does to Our Brains

Looking at addiction and hostile takeovers through the lens of science simultaneously gives us hope and scares the living daylights out of us. Addictions are runaway habits, and the problem with bad habits is that they create channels in our thought processes.

In other words, the more we do something, the more difficult it is to change our behavior the next time around. One of the most shocking discoveries in recent years is the concept of "brain remapping." Our behaviors—and the chemicals associated with those behaviors—alter how our brains function over time. Just as psychoactive drugs can deeply imprint emotional memories of euphoria or pain relief (what we might call addiction memories), so too do certain natural chemicals released in our brains imprint patterns and adjust cravings.

Extensive research in this area has been done on lab rats. (I mention it reluctantly, because I'm a bleeding-heart animal lover and even the stories make me sad. The results of the study are so significant, though, that I need to mention them.) Researchers hooked rats to electrodes that sent euphoric feelings into their brains every time they pushed a switch—similar to what a person would get from taking a drug like cocaine. Researchers found that the rats pushed it up to five thousand times per hour, wouldn't eat or sleep, stopped all other activity, and eventually died of thirst or starvation.[12]

Some addictions stimulate the orbitofrontal cortex of the brain so strongly that it convinces the mind that the drug or activity is more enjoyable than anything else, even to the degree of reducing the pleasure of normal activity. The rat study also showed that when euphoric feelings were coupled with certain behaviors, unlearning those behaviors became far more difficult. Feeding the addiction produced not only an emotional reaction but an actual altering of brain cells. A study showed that alteration occurs if an addictive action is repeated three or more times, but even one incredibly intense experience can cause a change in brain cells.[13] The additional complication is that most stimulations decrease over time, but the craving doesn't; therefore, we need more and more of the stimulant to get the same effect.

A Two-Pronged Assault

It bears repeating that all addictive processes have at least two crucial sides: physical and emotional. (I would argue there is a third, the spiritual, but I will leave this part out for now.) Any attempt to bring change must address both impact points. For smokers, the challenge to overcoming their addiction is not just the draw from nicotine but also the soothing hand-to-mouth pattern. For the sex addict, it's not only the endorphin rush but the pacification of frustration and numbing of emotional pain. Stimulant drug users struggle just as much with the chemicals as they do with the pattern of needing to perform and chasing after more. If we only treat one side of the problem, we will find less success and may give up when we don't progress.

HALT is a very helpful acronym for triggers. It stands for *hungry, angry, lonely,* and *tired.* Why would loneliness trigger a similar response as hunger, when one is a craving of the heart and the other is a physical craving? They connect with the physical and emotional sides of the addiction. This two-pronged assault is why addictions tend to come in bundles of both emotional chaos (broken relationships, denial, deceitfulness, avoidance, anxiety, depression) and physical deterioration (liver damage, lung cancer, insomnia, and so forth).

Leading a Revolution

Here's the good news: freedom is possible.

The road may be long and arduous. It will cost us. But millions of people are being set free through the help of the Lord, friends, family, medical professionals, and therapists. Addictions do not have to define or control us. But we must lead a revolution in our lives, and that begins with fighting back in our minds. We need a renewal of thinking about who God is and who we are in Him. We need to be reminded that we are more than conquerors with His power, victorious in Jesus Christ, not enslaved to our bodies' demands.

There's a right way to fight and a wrong way, a wise way, and a foolish way. We must let go of preconceived ideas about how we are made by God and what He may require of us. We need to open our eyes to our multifaceted design and learn how mind, will, emotions, spirit, soul, and body interplay

We Can't Wish Away Addiction

As human beings, we need to work with our nature and not just try to hope away our addictions. We must work with each part of our being as God intended. For the most part, we are to handle spiritual matters with spiritual tools, physical matters with physical tools, and emotional or mental matters with emotional or mental tools.

Unfortunately, we sometimes read Scripture with far too simple a lens. When we read passages like Galatians 5:16–24 and Colossians 3:5–10, we may see a simple command about needing to change our lives and then assume a simple solution, but that is not what the author meant. What do you see when you read these verses?

> But I say, *walk by the Spirit, and you will not gratify the desires of the flesh*. For the desires of the flesh are against the Spirit, and the desires of the Spirit are against the flesh, for these are opposed to each other, to keep you from doing the things you want to do. But if you are led by the Spirit, you are not under the law. . . . And *those who belong to Christ Jesus have crucified the flesh with its passions and desires.* (Gal. 5:16–18, 24)

> *Put to death therefore what is earthly in you*: sexual immorality, impurity, passion, evil desire, and covetousness, which is idolatry. On account of these the wrath of God is coming. In these

you too once walked, when you were living in them. But now you must put them all away: anger, wrath, malice, slander, and obscene talk from your mouth. Do not lie to one another, seeing that *you have put off the old self with its practices and have put on the new self, which is being renewed in knowledge after the image of its creator.* (Col. 3:5–10)

On the surface it looks easy, right? Paul seems to be saying, "Your lives are screwed up, so stop doing those things and turn it around. You are Christians, so why are you struggling at all? God made it easy for us to walk away from sin and bad behavior. Just start walking on the good road, and everything will be okay." Unfortunately, that is the misinformed perspective being preached in so many of the nation's pulpits. But is this what Paul meant?

Or was he saying, "These behaviors are dishonoring to the Lord and not a part of our new identities in Christ. Therefore, we need to do whatever is necessary to dig down and wisely root them out through whatever process God walks us through"? That process may be spiritual. But if our issues have physical and mental components, the process will be physical and mental as well. We would never read more devotions to heal from a hamstring injury. Nor would we dream of worshiping away bad hygiene. There are some things that need to be handled one way, some handled another. I am thankful the Lord has revealed more and more to us about how He made us and how we can steward our minds, hearts, and bodies.

How Do We Heal?

I am a man of prayer who believes in the supernatural healing of God. I have seen a few miraculous healings of addictions and have heard my fair share of testimonies about overnight freedom. I praise God for those accounts and believe them wholeheartedly.

The advice I give others is always to pray and seek the Lord for His healing until we hear a clear answer. So please hear that I'm not advocating an antisupernatural stance in any way. However, I want to affirm the understanding that we are complex ecosystems designed by God to be navigated as He intended. There's nothing wrong with asking God for a shortcut, but proper stewardship means we must be willing to put in the hard work as well.

Freedom from addiction begins with accurate theology. I believe God wants freedom from evil for all of His children. I believe He is more interested in full deliverance than in temporary rescue. I believe God wants to walk us through processes so we may appreciate the ramifications of our choices and because He wants us to own the process personally and deeply. I think He wants us to work hard to undo what the Devil did so that we grow a hatred for sin and the activity of the Enemy. I think that when we realize the depths to which we have fallen and observe a personal Lord guiding us out, His glory is maximized. Therefore, it's God's primary will to walk us out of the maze the same way we walked into the maze: step by step, decision by decision, day by day.

Second, I believe freedom from addiction is found in growing awareness and embracing our true identities in Christ. We are children of God. We are accepted and loved not because we perform well but because God chose to love us when we were unlovable. If we were wretches when He saved us, He's not shocked by our behavior now. If grace lifted us from the muck and mire, then grace will lead us home. If we have been taken from the kingdom of darkness and transported into the kingdom of light, as adopted children of the King, then we have new identities with new callings, new resources, new freedom, new power, and new authority. Behavior that used to make sense no longer does. We hold to that sense of identity in Christ as we look at how we can heal from addictions and hostile mental takeovers.

Taking the Promised Land

One day at a time.

That's a common phrase in twelve-step programs. While to the uninitiated it sounds cliché, to the recovering addict it sounds like a plan. To me it sounds like God's strategy of taking the Promised Land.

Most of us remember the conquest of the Promised Land as simple and quick. We remember Joshua beginning at Jericho, where God brought the walls down with just a shout, and ending with full victory a short time later.[14] But that's not how the story really went. Yes, the conquest of the land began with a miraculous supernatural victory at Jericho, but don't forget the immediate defeat at the next smaller city due to sin and poor decisions.[15] Yes, the Lord fought for Israel and carved out for them a Promised Land, but not without fits and starts, failures and doubts, losses and wins, and constant battles with stubborn enemies. God easily could have sent an army of angels to clear the path or destroyed the enemies with the sound of His voice, but He didn't. Why? Partly it was due to Israel's disobedience, but partly it was due to God's plans.[16]

Twice, Scripture—through the voice of Moses—records God's intentions for the Promised Land conquest. The Lord told the Israelites once at the beginning of their journey—along with delivering the Ten Commandments on Mount Sinai—and, as if He didn't want them to miss it, He repeated Himself later as Israel stood at the edge of Palestine. One critical, yet often forgotten, portion of the plan was the "little by little" part.

> I will not drive them out from before you in one year, lest the land become desolate and the wild beasts multiply against you. Little by little I will drive them out from before you, until you have increased and possess the land. (Ex. 23:29–30)

You shall not be in dread of them, for the LORD *your God is in your midst, a great and awesome God. The* LORD *your God will clear away these nations before you little by little. You may not make an end of them at once, lest the wild beasts grow too numerous for you.* But the LORD your God will give them over to you and throw them into great confusion, until they are destroyed. (Deut. 7:21–23)

Little by little.

Day by day.

The end result would be the same, but in these passages God spoke to process. Did you see the reason for it? It was for the Israelites—for their full ownership. God could have given them total victory all at once, but what would have happened? They didn't have time to expand their numbers through childbearing to fill the land they would have received, and the "wild beasts" would have backfilled in and hurt them. They would have lost the territory God gave them. Therefore, He cleared the way slowly, little by little, day by day, so they could own the land along the way and keep it once and for all.

God gives us a pathway to victory, a way out. Addiction is serious but not hopeless. Sometimes God helps us advance in quantum leaps, and other days He leads us as slowly as molasses. Usually, Jesus fixes things slowly or progressively because He is healing deeper layers than we are seeking help for. He is not stubbornly delaying the process; He is wisely doing all that the true process takes.

A Practical Process

We will deal with helps, tools, tricks, and insights on how to bring our minds back under our control and submit them to the Master in the last third of this book, so for now let me explain just a few of the practical process pieces of emerging from addiction.

Denial gets us nowhere. A cliché sitcom routine features a psychologist who says, "Admitting you have a problem is half the battle." It's true. As long as we aren't convinced hostile takeover is a serious issue, we will not put in the effort required for victory. Falling at the feet of the cross again and again and admitting we are broken and in need keeps us squarely on the path of health.

We cannot do it alone. God built us to interact with community. We are relational, and walking the road out of addiction alone is to almost assure failure. We need other perspectives, encouragement, truth speakers, reliable guides, shoulders to lean on, and ears to listen. The greatest chain of addiction that Satan binds us with is secret isolation. To fully defeat an addiction, we must bring it out into the light and address it in safe community.

Three of the four Gospels of the New Testament tell a story of a paralyzed man brought before Jesus. Because he couldn't walk, his friends carried him to the house where Jesus was ministering. Unable to find a way in due to the crowds, they went up on the roof and dug through the ceiling, eventually lowering the man down before the Lord. Graciously, Christ not only forgave his sins, ministering to his soul, but healed his body as well. The man left walking and praising God.

That man would have never seen Jesus if his friends hadn't carried him there.

Sometimes we need to be carried out of our addiction because we cannot walk out of our own volition. If our wills have been obliterated by significant and long-standing bondage, we may not be able to get out on our own. It's then that we need to suck up our pride and let our friends carry us to safety.

We shouldn't simply trade one addiction for another. How many recovery groups have to take a smoke break? Even the smokers' recovery groups have to have coffee. Simply trading one bondage for another isn't the health we are looking for. We may feel that we are downgrading the seriousness of the addiction (from heroin to methadone, for example), but we must remind ourselves we aren't looking for looser or weaker chains. We are looking for empty wrists. Merely finding another way of escaping our problems doesn't fix them. We must get to the root, what's underneath it all, and repair there.

Addiction and hostile takeover are not the end of the story. As we allow the Lord to bring light to the situation and power for breakthrough, and as we renew our minds to right thinking, freedom is probable. Jesus Christ can set us free. The Holy Spirit is more than capable of bringing our minds back in line with His.

Yet we must be willing to take a look at our lives with honesty and clarity. We can only grow from where we really are, not where we wish to be.

Chapter 8

The Land of Make-Believe

W e've looked at who we are in God's eyes and how that should affect how we think. Then we examined various barriers to that right mind-set—the world, the flesh, the Devil—and giving in to temptations, sin, compulsions, and addictions. In the next chapter we'll discuss key solutions for transforming our thinking for the mastering of our minds, but first we'll talk about one last barrier: our tendency to live in a fantasy world instead of seeing what is real.

Everybody remembers *Mister Rogers' Neighborhood*, right? The show where an overly nice guy changes his shoes and sweater once he gets home from work and talks super gently to kids about the world while he feeds his fish and talks with random neighbors who drop by? Sure we do. But did you know that it aired from 1968 to 2001, produced 895 episodes, and earned four Emmy awards? Holy cow! Did you also know that Mister Rogers's mother's maiden name was McFeely? Or that the original fish were called Fennel and Frieda?

It's impossible to remember that show without remembering the trips via trolley to the Neighborhood of Make-Believe. There,

King Friday XIII and his wife, Queen Sara Saturday (named after Rogers's wife), ran their kingdom inhabited by Henrietta Pussycat, X the Owl, and Daniel Striped Tiger. As uncomfortable as I was with the king's and queen's puppet heads, it was really Lady Elaine Fairchilde who freaked me out the most, probably due to seeing too many horror movies that involved dolls. Yet I don't want to dishonor the sweet show and the incredible transformation that Fred Rogers led in the lives of children nationwide. There's a reason that a Presbyterian reverend from Pennsylvania received the coveted Peabody Award, the Ralph Lowell Award, more than forty honorary degrees, and the Presidential Medal of Freedom. He's *the man*.

Rogers purposely used the Neighborhood of Make-Believe to talk more extensively about important issues. He wanted to use children's imaginations as God intended them—to think through new perspectives. He did his best to keep make-believe separate from reality and not confuse the kids, believing that all children deserved the honor of being talked to honestly and forthrightly.

In contrast to these clean lines of demarcation between imagination and reality, illusionists and magicians purposely distort reality and blur the lines for entertainment. I'm not saying that's bad; I love illusions and magic tricks. In fact, I was a big fan of the short-lived show *Mindfreak*, by illusionist and showman Criss Angel, and I have always found street magician and endurance artist David Blaine to be incredible. A number of years ago, my daughters and I watched as many rerun episodes of *Breaking the Magician's Code: Magic's Biggest Secrets Finally Revealed* as we could, equally impressed by the art of the deception and the illusion experience itself. In the show a "masked magician" exposed how the most famous illusions and magic tricks are done. For example, we learned that the famous "sawing a woman in half" trick is much more about the woman's ability to contort her body in the box and hide in very small areas than it is about any sort of magic. The use of perfectly placed mirrors, brilliant sleight of hand, and impeccable timing with distraction is awe-inspiring.

But the movie *The Matrix* is what really raised deeper questions for me about real versus unreal. I don't want to spend too much time on this movie because it's been used as illustration fodder for far too long, so I'll just touch on it briefly. The film follows the story of a computer hacker, Thomas Anderson, who goes by the online name Neo. He is approached by a group of futuristic-looking people and invited to see what life is all about. He is offered a blue pill and a red pill. One will let him forget the whole thing, and the other will take him down the Alice in Wonderland rabbit hole into true reality. He opts for the journey and discovers that the life he's experiencing is not real—it's a computer program designed by the bad guys to keep the human race in line. Everything he knows is fake and fabricated. Only when Neo is truly awakened does he see how illusory his world has been and how harsh, real, and dangerous true life is.

It's an important question we need to grapple with: What's real?

I think we live too much of our lives up in our heads and spend too much energy living in fantasy. We fear imaginary scenarios. We long for fantasy solutions and futures. We live and have relationships online, never revealing our true selves or fully encountering others.

Many of the worlds we create in our minds simply aren't true. They aren't based in reality—at least not God's reality. Therefore, they tend to steal us away from what God desires for us and what He built us for. In this chapter I want to do what the masked magician did: expose the tricks. I want to hunt for clarity and call out what I believe is dangerous, fantastical living and thinking. I want to get us to the place where we fight the real battles that need to be fought, engage with the real struggles before us, embrace the real truths and tools of God, and live the lives that really need to be lived.

Instead of being led blindly into a world where the Enemy pretends to reign and negatively rules the day, I want us to be sure of God's love for us and His presence in our lives. I want us to be confident in the Holy Spirit's power to set us free. I want us to develop healthy reactions to struggles we face. I want us to be patient with the process. I want us to be secure in our identities, with thoughts filled with strength, health, joy, and peace. Life is filled with challenges—some legitimate and some completely imaginary. I don't want any of us carrying burdens we don't need to carry.

Those burdens can come from either good or bad fantasy. Negative fantasy—worrying about things that will never come to pass—dominates our minds and steals our energy. Positive fantasy—engrossing ourselves in fake worlds we think are better than the real one—steals our contentment and generates impossible dreams. Both cause problems.

Built for Glory; Soured by Lies

If we are made in the image of God, and His likeness emanates through us, then we were designed for glory. If God, a master artist and creative genius, made this world out of nothing, then this world is filled with evidence of His greatness. If He gives us each breath, sends the soothing wind on a hot day, teaches us how to build things to make life easier, populates the planet with community, and shows us how to love, then He is worthy of praise. So why don't we praise Him more? Why aren't we more thankful? Why do our hearts not burst with gratitude?

We have been lied to.

We have been taught that this world should be something other than what it is. We have become convinced that God could make it better but refuses because He doesn't think we are worth it. We are told there is a land of candy, treats, sex, fame, fun, money, power, and control where we will be treated like the kings and queens we are, if only we will take hold of it and choose another way.

Those fantasies are lies.

It's the role of Christians to follow the Lord out of Fantasyland and back into the real kingdom of light He built for us. The Holy Spirit was sent to us as a guide, one who would lead us into all truth. He walks alongside us and helps us discern fact from fiction. And when we see the guideposts of honesty He illuminates, it's our job to call out to one another and shout the way to freedom.

When Jesus Christ called Saul of Tarsus (the apostle Paul) on the road to Damascus, He specifically called him to preach to the Gentiles a message of truth to lead them away from the lies of the Enemy. Paul told it like this:

> And *the Lord said, "I am Jesus* whom you are persecuting. But rise and stand upon your feet, for *I have appeared to you for this purpose, to appoint you as a servant and witness* to the things in which you have seen me and to those in which I will appear to you, delivering you from your people and from the Gentiles—to whom I am sending you *to open their eyes, so that they may turn from darkness to light and from the power of Satan to God,* that they may receive forgiveness of sins and a place among those who are sanctified by faith in me." (Acts 26:15–18)

It's no wonder that when Paul gave advice to the churches he planted, he spoke freely of exposing the lies of the Enemy "so that we would not be outwitted by Satan; for we are not ignorant of his designs" (2 Cor. 2:11).

Just as looking behind the curtain of a magic trick reveals a painfully obvious setup we are shocked to have missed, so too does the Bible reveal the lies we buy and sell every day.

The Most Dangerous Fantasies

Let me begin with a disclaimer: I'm likely the worst fantasy offender in the room. I live in my head more than anyone I know. Because I have panic disorder, my fear comes from a place of irrationality and is not based in reality. All of my escapism is thought-based and dream-based. In fact, my depth of fantasy almost stopped me from writing this chapter—and even this book—because I didn't feel I've had enough victory in this area of my life. I continued because I wanted you to hear this information from the mouth of someone who truly struggles, just like you.

Although all thoughts not created by God are by definition dangerous, I want to highlight a few fantasies that have become popular in today's world.

Fantasy Fear

We are afraid of a lot of things that don't exist. Like children who get freaked out by ghost stories around the campfire, we run from shadows. We are scared of the dark, scared of the unknown, scared of different, scared of mystery, scared of not being fully informed, scared of what-ifs, scared of tomorrow, scared of the supernatural, scared of failure, and, ultimately, scared of death.

Do you know how horror movies are made? One how-to-make-horror-movies website says,

> Know that the evils we don't see are scarier than the ones we can. The human imagination will almost always conjure up a scarier image than you can show on the screen. Why? Because each person will fill in the images that scare them the most. This is why, in the beginnings of most horror movies, you only get fleeting glimpses of the evil that is lurking in the corners. . . .

Horror is about fear of the unknown—so let the audience sit in the dark for as long as possible.[1]

Whether it's Jason from *Friday the 13th* in a hockey mask or scarred Freddy Krueger in *A Nightmare on Elm Street*, horror-movie villains are only scary in small doses, with a lot of unanticipated jump scares and plenty of dark shadows. Imagine how un-scary it would be if Michael Myers, the killer from *Halloween*, was simply walking in broad daylight down the street or shopping at Walmart. In fact, it was not seeing the creature that made *Cloverfield* interesting and director M. Night Shyamalan's blockbuster hit *Signs* so freaky.

Suspension of belief also makes a movie scary. That means pretending that completely unrealistic things can happen, instead of feeling jarred out of the story. Imagine how frustrating it would be for the monster to hide in the closet for eight hours while the victim was at work and then decided to do a little overtime. What was he doing in there? How many times did the serial killer have to use the restroom while he was waiting, and did he wash his hands? What's scary is the fantasy that the monster and the serial killer were in the closet at the exact right time doing terribly creepy things just before they needed to jump out. It's not scary if real life enters the equation.

God knows what we need and what we don't need. God equipped us with everything we need to fight real enemies, not fake ones. We do not have the strength to fight imagined all-powerful enemies because we don't need it; they don't exist. God deals in the real and lives in the light. In the light, shadows are forced away, and we see things for what they truly are. Once we see reality, we can find the appropriate power and authority, given to us by our Father, to face it.

Fantasy Expectations

We have been programmed to chase the elusive. We long for things that will never be. For example, we work our hearts out in a rat race that has no winners. Our insecurities compel us to perform, believing that the end of the race is just around the corner, but it's not. We think that if we keep going just one more week we will arrive, but behind the immediate hill is a higher and steeper hill. This life was never designed to arrive. It's designed for process, and learning, growing, and transforming are all built into it. The reason we need heaven is that this life will always fall short.

Unfortunately, modern-day America has wholeheartedly bought in to the rat race, which we are now living at a pace we can't sustain. Once we designed a world that could replace the cycles of nature (i.e., the light bulb replaced the sun cycle), we stepped away from how God designed us and began to make a world that's impossible to navigate.

Each time we are disappointed with how our lives are shaping up compared to our expectations, we blame God. We figure that He should equip us with the ability to easily rise above our circumstances regardless of the changes we have made to our world. But what if God's original design for us was perfect for the world He created, and we are making changes we aren't supposed to be able to handle? What if we are living beyond His intentions? Is it His fault or ours?

Fantasy Fulfillment

We also wrestle with fantasy fulfillment. Not only are we disappointed with tomorrow but we already rue today. We wait and wait for the perfect to come. We have been trained to believe that perfect is possible—but it's not. We spend our young adult years searching for "the one"—the perfect person to marry—but "the one" doesn't exist, and divorce rates continue to climb. More and more couples separate because they are unfulfilled in their marriages, only to find that it's twice as hard to make a second marriage work. Statistics for third marriages are dismal.

We get pop-ups on our computers telling us that the perfect job is out there, but that only makes us more critical of the job we have now. Movies show characters living amazingly fulfilled lives, and that increases our bitterness about our current situations. We wait and wait and wait. Meanwhile, our disappointment makes us sad. We cry out to God or anyone who will listen for more and better, but we hear nothing in return. Eventually the pain of *now* drives us to live out of the moment and in the imaginary tomorrow.

When I was about thirteen years old, a family member bought me a trilogy of fantasy books called Dragonlance. Clearly, she selected it due to my name and thought I would like it because of my love for the mythical. It's hard to have the nickname Lancelot and not be interested in knights, dragons, and wizards. I read the first book and was immediately entranced. It was full of adventure and easy to read, with captivating story lines and fun characters. I was hooked. I quickly finished the first book and dove into the second.

At the same time, my real life was difficult. I was still reeling from my parents' divorce six years prior. I was disappointed with life, fearful and anxious, struggling with school, and trying to wrap my mind around God's expectations of me. The fantasy world of Dragonlance was my escape. I couldn't wait to get home and start reading. I read slowly so I could milk all of the goodness out of the books. I didn't want them to end. I didn't know at the time that Dragonlance would become a huge, best-selling series with more books than I could read in half a decade. I thought there would be only three, and I didn't want to let the fantasy world go.

Eventually I found myself beginning to change. I started wanting to be in the book more than in real life. I didn't want to talk to people as much as I wanted to read about imaginary conversations. I didn't want to go anywhere as much as I wanted to read about people going to magical lands. It got so bad that at the age of fourteen, when I was halfway through the third book of the series, I put it down and never picked it back up. Even as a teen, I knew I was slipping. I wasn't healthy. I wanted fantasy far more than reality, and that scared me.

"Reality TV" has been filling our airwaves since the nineties, and enough scandals, exposés, and stories have come out to reveal just how "un-real" it is. Yet some of us still believe that all the stars live dreamy lives and all the wealthy throw lavish feasts with a hundred of their best friends and dance every night away. But what is not shown is far more real than what is shown. Even the bad stuff on reality shows is mostly faked. Many scenes are reenacted by the cast members in order to capture the drama on camera. What may have started as real is quickly redesigned as a fake. If we had a genuine reality television show, it would be so boring that no one would watch. Real life is ordinary.

We want to dream. We want to pretend that there is a better life where we can be truly happy all the time. We want to be fooled. We want to escape our disappointment. We simply can't believe that this is all there is to life. We hold out hope because we've been trained to believe that this isn't enough. The more we are exposed to on social media and TV, the more we realize how much we lack. Nothing measures up anymore. Our cars aren't fast enough, our spouses aren't hot enough, our kids aren't good enough, our wallets aren't fat enough, our houses aren't big enough, our dogs aren't cute enough, our bodies aren't beautiful enough, our minds aren't smart enough, our churches aren't impressive enough, our schools aren't doing enough, our jobs aren't interesting enough, and our futures aren't bright enough.

How is a soul to rest—and how is God supposed to be praised—in a world like that?

Are we entitled to a better existence? Is it all about me? Are we being let down? The problem with all of those questions is that despite the answers we come up with, all the questions are coming from a self-obsessed place. When the "I" becomes king, we all become slaves. We think we are empowering ourselves, but in fact we are diminishing our power with every selfish thought and act.

Religious Fantasy

Even our faith isn't safe from fantastical thinking. God has shown us through Scripture who He is and what is important to Him, but often we ignore that and decide what we want Him to be like. When we do that, we're believing in a fantasy God.

Consider this hilarious story in the New Testament book of Acts:

When Paul had gathered a bundle of sticks and put them on the fire, a viper came out because of the heat and fastened on his hand. *When the native people saw the creature hanging from his hand, they said to one another, "No doubt this man is a murderer. Though he has escaped from the sea, Justice has not allowed him to live."* He, however, shook off the creature into the fire and suffered no harm. They were waiting for him to swell up or suddenly fall down dead. *But when they had waited a long time and saw no misfortune come to him, they changed their minds and said that he was a god.* (Acts 28:3–6)[2]

So is Paul a murderer or a god?

How easily they slid from one opinion to another. The people of Malta had their preconceived ideas about who God was and how He acted. In their religious fantasy, the gods punished—so they first saw the snake as an act of retribution. After Paul was unharmed, they didn't know what to think. Rather than considering that maybe their view of God was wrong, they concluded that Paul himself must be a god. That was the only thing that made sense to them.

It's easy to cast blame on those "ignorant" people in the story. But how much blame needs to stick with us when it comes to treating Christianity like superstition and magic? How many of us pray to God as though He is a cosmic vending machine? How many of us think that God will do bad things to us unless we remain vigilant in doing right? How many of us wait for "the other shoe to drop," sure that God will be ready to bring us down if our lives are going too well? How many of us think that God should do more things for us if we are good little kids? Don't we all fall for the trap of thinking our prayers will be answered more often if we use all the right words? What about the temptation to use religious items as a talisman or protector? All of those scenarios cross over into superstition and magical thinking.

God is a Person, not a force. Faith is trust, not mind control. Christianity is a relationship, not a system. Discipleship is duplicating the life of Christ, not memorizing the right trivia. Prayer is communication, not a set of mantras. I think you get my point. We must continue to resist the temptation to live Christian lives apart from how they were designed by God Himself. We must remain fixed on what He laid down in the Bible and through the life of Christ as an example of true religion.

Return of the Living Dead—Practical Helps

So how do we break the power of fantasy in our lives? How do we tighten our grip on reality? Here are a few practical helps.

Back on Planet Earth

God shaped us specifically to live on this planet. He did not build us for fantasy realms. He didn't equip us for imaginary adventures. He empowers us for real struggles, real temptations, real difficulties, real pain, real fear, real grief, real doubt, real trials, and real existence. Once we are called to heaven, we will be redesigned to live there and live by those rules, but for now we need to engage with *here*. I spend most of my mental energy living in supernatural realms and the exponentially expanding world of "what if." I hear the whisper of God constantly calling me back to look at the trees He built, feel the wind He blows, work the jobs He brings, and engage with the people He's put around me. When our lives here are done, we will never come back to this planet again. Once we are gone, we are gone. There is a unique measure of glory to be given to God for this planet, this place, this time, that once we are in heaven cannot be given. God deserves all the glory for all He does in the here and now, not just for an imaginary future.

Learning the Secret to Contentment

Paul gave advice about contentment to the ancient church in Philippi (modern-day Greece), but he may as well have been writing to us today in the USA. He said, "Not that I am speaking of being in need, for *I have learned in whatever situation I am to be content. I know how to be brought low, and I know how to abound. In any and every circumstance, I have learned the secret* of facing plenty and hunger, abundance and need. I can do all things through him who strengthens me" (Phil. 4:11–13).

At the heart of fantasy is the belief that our current reality isn't good enough. The more intense the discontent, the more we have bought into the lie that there is more out there being withheld from us. Yet how much of the state of our hearts is simply a matter of perspective? How much is *enough*? Would more really change our circumstances? There are poor families far happier and more content than wealthy families. There are people with cancer peacefully surrounded by family, while healthy millionaire executives sit lonely in their high-rise offices. Blessing can be found in both abundance and lack.

Think back to the rich times in your life, the times when you grew, when truth found its way to your heart, when life deepened. Were they all positive experiences? Were they all negative? Or is it a blend? Wasn't your wedding day especially joyful and the beauty of welcoming your first baby into the world overwhelming? Wasn't rallying the family around Grandma's casket unifying and right? Wasn't there value in both the laughter and heartache of middle school? Can't we have fun with both a simple jump rope and a Ferrari? Is it the thing that determines the contentment, or is it the heart that receives the thing? Is it the circumstance that determines the joy, or is it the mind-set that walked into it?

My friend Pastor Brian Kiley says, "When you believe you are entitled to nothing, everything is a blessing." Brilliant. When we can tune our minds into a channel of contentment, every experience of life takes on the tone of joy. We must remind ourselves of what God *has* done and what He *is* doing, and hang on to the hope of what He promised to do.

Restoring a Heart of Gratitude

God deserves praise, and we need to be thankful people. Yet it's so easy to lose our grip on gratitude and thanksgiving. How many First World visitors have seen the extreme poverty in Calcutta, India, and returned home stunned at the opulence and abundance of where they live—only to recede back into greed weeks later? How many of us have refused to give praise to our heavenly Father because His gift fell below our expectations? How many of us would have made it through the wilderness exodus journey with

Moses without getting judged for grumbling? Ingratitude is an offense to God. Falling prey to the "grass is greener" syndrome is an insult to the farmer who prepared the grass we are standing on.

Thanksgiving is a chosen mind-set. We have to determine how we are going to see things—whether we are going to be "glass is half empty" or "glass is half full" types of people. All my life I have been teased for being a bit of a Pollyanna, or too positive. I have been called unrealistic and been snickered at for having my head in the clouds. Maybe some of that assessment was accurate, but I determined early on in life that I would force myself to see the positive every day. I didn't want be dour and negative. A positive mind-set of thanksgiving is a lifelong discipline for me.

It's easy to fall into negative patterns of thinking. It's easy to be mad and bitter. A more honorable challenge is to be the one who clings to the hope of Christ in all circumstances and always looks around the corner for the Lord's rescue.

God's way and God's mind-set are the most realistic. There's nothing more real than God, nothing more real than heaven.

Necessary Mind Games

When we are trying to grow into a role, we may find ourselves pretending at first. Like little kids trying on their parents' clothes that they will eventually grow into, we need to try on thoughts and attitudes that will eventually fit us and feel normal as we mature in our relationship with God. Sometimes we need to believe things that seem unrealistic but God says are accurate. Sometimes we need to lift our eyes above what's right in front of us (like Peter when he was afraid of the waves) so that we can keep our hearts aligned with His (focused on the eyes of Jesus). Contrary to what we might see and feel in any given moment, we need to live as though God loves us and accepts us as His children. As though we are forgiven and free. As though God listens to our prayers. As though grace matters. As though God is on the throne, ruling this world from on high. As though our identities are tied to Christ, not to what we do for a living or what other people say we are. As though eternal life begins today, not just when we die. As though Christ defeated death and there is no more bondage to fear.

Isn't this type of mind game just more fantasy thinking? It's a fair question, but the answer is no. That's because everything God says and promises is true. Our current mind-set is fantasy, and we are trying to break out into reality. Pretending our way into reality is an appropriate use of our imagination as God designed it. Before NASA launched the first man to the moon, someone imagined that it was possible. Before Everest was climbed, someone dreamed that it could be done. Before love stirred, someone hoped that it might. We need to believe what's right until our lives align with it.

> There are three stages to every great work of God; first it
> is impossible, then it is difficult, then it is done . . . God's
> work done in God's way will never lack God's supply.
> —JAMES HUDSON TAYLOR

Chapter 9

All Hail the King

Have you ever driven across America and seen the vast array of our beautiful country's landscapes?

In 1993, I had that incredible opportunity as a twenty-one-year-old traveling on a small, self-organized tour in a Christian heavy metal band called Jesus Freaks. We thought it would be a great idea to buy an old "Minnie-Winnie" Winnebago, put four grown men in it, and live on the road for three and a half months with no money except what we earned in T-shirt and CD sales. Did I mention we did it in the winter? We started from Sacramento and went south through Redondo Beach, deep down into Corpus Christi, up into Michigan, across to Niagara Falls, into the New England states, and then all the way down the East Coast into Georgia and Alabama.

I learned four things about the United States through that experience:

1. We live in a big, incredible country.
2. It's not so big that you can't drive across it and see it all. That trip made it somehow feel bigger and smaller at the same time.

3. We have very distinct cultures across our nation, but the heart of people remains the same.

4. The greenery of eastern Washington State and the rolling hills of Kentucky bluegrass, where horses roamed the land, visually impressed me the most.

That trip also made me wonder why I was taught in school that America was overcrowded, yet I drove hours and hours through empty land with not a soul in sight. It made me wonder what the country looked like before we transformed it all into agricultural and commercial land. I also wondered if the dream of picking up and settling into an unowned part of the nation—to make it yours, to set up a new life, and to claim new territory—was real.

And then I did the research.

There is no unowned land in the United States. There might be uninhabited, unclaimed, or abandoned land, but no land is officially without an owner. People argue squatter's rights and miner's rights, but, practically speaking, there is no unowned land in America; it's all owned by the government if not by an individual. There is even some argument about whether unowned land exists anywhere in the world. Some people suggest that Antarctica doesn't seem to have an official owner. The reason? It's a wasteland. No one cares. There's nothing there for someone to take. You can be assured that anything of value will be claimed quickly.

You and I are precious—and so is every other human on earth. No soul on the planet is unclaimed. If we're believers, our hearts have been bought by Jesus Christ. But in some cases we have abandoned the territory He claimed, and now Satan is squatting on it. Either way, no one is free.

It's always been that way. Only two people on earth have ever been truly free and relatively unclaimed: Adam and Eve. God formed them, breathed life into them, and set them free into the world. He could have made them His slaves and forced them to manage His creation, but He didn't. He longed for their love and loyalty, so He made them free. He had their hearts for a while, until the Devil came along with his doubt and his options. On the day Adam and Eve ate the fruit, they sold their souls to the Enemy. He's been claiming ownership over mankind ever since.

One of the greatest fallacies we believe is that we are independent beings in charge of our own lives. We take pride in being "self-made" and independent, but nothing could be further from the truth. We think that freedom means living completely on our own terms, by our own power. We are not equipped for that. In a world of superbeings like God, the Devil, angels, and demons, who are all extraordinarily complex and brilliant, our tiny brains and wills will never be fully in control of our lives. We are as vulnerable as a newborn baby.

Jesus Christ needed to come to set us free. We are free to become what He created us to be and not be forced into the mold of our enemies. True freedom is the ability to live out our created intent. Freedom does not mean the allowance to re-create ourselves into something we are not; it means that finally we are able to express our real identities without the crushing weight of sin and the pressures of evil.[1]

Our Master paid for us. He broke the control of the bad guys, paid the price for our sins, and released us once again to love Him the way He wished Adam and Eve would have.[2] But make no mistake: we cannot live truly autonomously.[3]

Allegiance to no one is allegiance to self, and self cannot save.[4] Even if we are free, we still need a Savior.[5] We are still designed for relationship with God as our Father. We are still built for His glory. We are not our own.

We crave to follow someone and be owned. We long to worship. We want someone to care for us, protect us, and make us have more than we would alone. On the road of life, we are not walking alone. There are companions, voices, suggestions, attractions, lures, whispers, and downright bullies that want to own us. Most of us didn't get two steps down the path before we sold out.[6]

Who owns you?[7]

I pray that it's our Lord and Savior Jesus Christ, the King of all creation.

He owns me three times over: He first formed me in my mother's womb[8] as my Creator. Second, He bought me back on the cross.[9] Third, I pledged myself to Him as a six-year-old at the altar of First Assembly of God in Roseville, California, in 1977.[10] I have since tried to live my life as an honorable and worthy servant/slave of my King.[11] No matter how much I have failed along the way, I still belong to Him, as 1 Corinthians reminds us: "Or do you not know that your body is a temple of the Holy Spirit within you, whom you have from God? *You are not your own, for you were bought with a price. So glorify God in your body*" (6:19–20).

There are three great truths in these two verses. One speaks of Christ purchasing us back, or redeeming us, from our sins on the cross. The second reveals that we are the temple of the Holy Spirit, meaning that the presence of God Himself dwells within us. The third shares that we have the ability to glorify God, make Him look good, and honor Him by how we treat our bodies and minds. We are His, and He says that we matter. What we do with our minds directly affects how God is able to reveal Himself to the world.

Who Owns the Property Rights to Our Minds?

Jesus bought it; Jesus owns it.

It was His to begin with, and it's His again.

If you buy land, you get to determine what goes on it. If you buy a car, you decide where it goes. If you buy a house, you can paint it the color of your choosing (barring absurd neighborhood regulations). If you own something, it's yours to do with what you please. You alone have the right to determine its use.

God has more than just ownership of our minds; it's kingship. A king holds not only the deed to his land but the authority to dictate actions upon that land that may or may not make the owner very happy or even benefit the owner directly. God is the monarch of our minds.

God alone has the right to determine what's in our minds and how we use them. Much like an embassy in a different country, our minds are God's territory in a foreign land. When the United States has an embassy in another country, that space, those grounds (although maybe not the actual dirt under them), that sphere of influence is under the control and direction of the United States—regardless of what country it is in and what the local laws are. Even if the activity around it and the people engaging with it are foreign, the embassy is a mini United States operated by the rules of the United States. According to the US Department of State, "While diplomatic spaces remain the territory of the host state, an embassy or consulate represents a sovereign state. International rules do not allow representatives of the host country to enter an embassy without permission—even to put out a fire—and designate an attack on an embassy as an attack on the country it represents."[12]

I may be a little too swayed by spy movies from Hollywood, but that last line of definition caught my attention: "an attack on an embassy [is considered] an attack on the country it represents." That means if an angry mob in Kabul rages against the US Embassy there, it's like they're attacking our soil. A 2013 report by the US Department of State, Bureau of Diplomatic Security, listed 272 separate "significant attacks against U.S. Diplomatic Facilities and Personnel" in a fifteen-year span (1998–2012). Perhaps one of the most famous attacks on a foreign-based US compound was the 2012 assault in Benghazi, Libya, that took the life of ambassador J. Christopher Stevens and US foreign service information management officer Sean Smith along with two CIA operatives, former Navy SEALs Glen Doherty and Tyrone Woods. It doesn't matter that this occurred in Libya; it was seen as an attack on America.

When our enemies (the world, the flesh, and the Devil) attack us, God takes it personally. He is twice attacked—once on His own land He purchased through the death of His Son, and again when the precious children He loves are harmed. The church is called the body of Christ for a reason: we are an extension of Him, indwelt by Him, a part of Him. That is why when Saul of Tarsus (later the apostle Paul) was stopped by Jesus Christ on the road to Damascus as he went there to persecute Christians, Jesus said, "'Saul, Saul, *why are you persecuting me?*' And [Saul] said, 'Who are you, Lord?' And he said, *'I am Jesus, whom you are persecuting*'" (Acts 9:4–5).

Saul was putting Christians in prison so they might be executed for being "Followers of the Way." So why did Jesus say that Paul was persecuting Him personally? Because not only are we God's family and the most cherished possessions of His heart, but we are His territory. An attack on us is an attack on Him.

Jesus paid a precious price for us. We will never know the full cost He paid on the cross, but our imaginations can get us partway there. Too many people think only of the physical suffering He endured but ignore His infinitely greater emotional and spiritual suffering. No one pays that much for something and then doesn't care how it's treated. No one suffers to that degree and lets the object of his affection out of his sight. No one does the unthinkable and then forgets. Jesus cares what happens in our minds because they belong to Him. And because of His ownership, He has the right to expect us to act a certain way, adhere to His rules, and submit to His process. Yet even if He didn't have expectations, wouldn't it be appropriate for us to live under the obligation of such a great love?

All In

If only we were singly focused—but we are not. We live in a self-designed world where agreeing with society allows us to believe and behave in contradictory ways. We try as hard as we can to live on the fence and play in both playgrounds. But God knows. He knows where our allegiance lies. He knows our hearts, our motives, and our intentions. He knows we are living a lie. Yet He refuses to give up on us, so He continues to call us back to what He made us to be, what He set us free for: a focused mind in alignment with His.

Over and over, Scripture tells us that we have to make a choice: we cannot serve two masters. We will love either one or the other.[13] There cannot be two kings. Either one rules or the other does. Christ said we are either for Him or against Him, gathering together or scattering abroad.[14] Yet we want to carry multiple banners, pretending that we are representing all the different groups, nations, and gods. We want to give a little of our hearts here, a little of our minds there. We want to spread the love to both our spouses and our mistresses. Yet we do not realize that loyalty to one means disloyalty to another.

God desires loyalty and faithfulness.[15] Those qualities are growing rarer and rarer as we are bombarded with options and becoming increasingly commitment phobic, but that doesn't change what God wants from us. Just because our postmodern culture chooses to fall prey to double-mindedness, inconsistency, and the trap of philosophical relativity doesn't mean that we must. We can choose to serve our king wholeheartedly. Faithfulness and single-mindedness come with a blessing. They're what our heavenly Father wants and how He built us to thrive.

One of the clearest examples recorded for us in the Bible of living in full alignment with and submission to God is a young virgin named Mary. I'm sure you know the Christmas story, but let me recap briefly. An angel visited a young woman in ancient Israel, a "nobody" by all accounts. The angel told her that the Holy Spirit would place a baby in her, and that child would be the incarnation of the Son of God and grow up to be the Savior of the world. As glorious as that sounds when we romanticize the story, the reality was brutal. This young lady, perhaps no more than fourteen to sixteen years old, was suddenly thrust into chaos. She faced immediate suspicion, rejection, and possibly expulsion from the community or even death. The rejection would come not only from her fiancé, Joseph (after all, who would believe a story like that?), but from her entire culture, which severely looked down on having children out of wedlock.

In one conversation, all of her dreams shattered. The white picket fence, the chatting with other young moms about baby stuff, the little boy who would look just like Joseph and be the pride of her family—it was all gone. She didn't even get to warm up to marriage before she faced being a mom. Alone and frightened, she tried to take in all that the angel was saying. After he finished, she replied, "Behold, I am the servant of the Lord; let it be to me according to your word" (Luke 1:38).

Are you kidding me?

Is that how you would have reacted as a teenager to news like that? Would you react like that today? Me neither.

How did Mary have the presence of mind, posture of heart, and submission of spirit to answer that way and mean it?

She knew who God was, and she knew who she was.

God was her King. She was His servant. Therefore, His plans were the only ones that mattered.

It Always Comes Back to Identity

I cannot say it enough: identity is at the heart of Christianity and at the heart of our lives. It's not a thing; it's *the* thing. As Christians, we do not have to navigate and climb a complex religious system. We don't earn our salvations or perform to be accepted by God. We don't struggle to gain righteousness. We can't do any of those things. We were helpless, drowning victims in need of rescue. Driven by love, God swooped down, lifted us up out of the water in His embrace, and set us on dry land with sweetness in His eyes. The rest of our Christian lives is about learning to understand His heart of love and living out what that means.

We reveal our true and designed identities by discovering who we are in light of who God is and what He has done. The Bible says that Jesus paid it all on the cross and that He said, "It is finished," before He died. Therefore, all the important stuff is done. We have nothing to add to the equation. In one act, Jesus gave us the right to become sons and daughters of God—to be reborn, adopted into the family of God, filled with the indwelling Holy Spirit, given a new identity. The rest of our existences flesh out the ramifications of that.

We are children of God.

He is the owner of our minds.

He is the King of our hearts.

He is our Father.

A Better Reason for Resistance

Unfortunately, many of us need to be convinced to live free and healthy as God's children. So many of us are content living with less. For some of us, it's because of laziness; for others, it comes from never being told that there was something better or that we had value. Yet certainly all of us can be blinded by the Enemy—not just about our identity in Christ but also about why we should resist losing ground that Christ has won for us. We are so used to living in bondage that we don't even bother fighting for ourselves.[16]

If we won't fight for ourselves, will we fight for Jesus?

Will we fight for our Savior?

Will we fight for our King?

Will we fight for our Father?

Will we allow His love to compel us to take a stand and fight back against the attacks upon our minds, souls, and identities? Will we respect and fear Him enough to present our bodies to Him—submitted, orderly, and healthy—as living sacrifices by using the power the Holy Spirit provides?[17] Will our love and gratitude be enough to fix our minds securely on Him and knit our hearts with His?

Is there a more noble reason to master our minds than to give them to the Master as an offering?

Alignment with God's Reality

We have not been offered a challenge with no instructions. We have not been commanded without an example. We are not only guessing as to what the Father expects of us when it comes to our minds and thoughts. We are told in no uncertain terms that we are to think like God and master our thoughts as Christ did.[18] Children take after their parents, and we are children of God. When we are saved, it is natural for us to think and be like our heavenly Father.

So what is the mind of God like? Although God's thoughts are above our thoughts and His ways are not our ways,[19] Scripture helps us determine a few things to emulate:

- God's mind is steady, consistent, cohesive, and filled with integrity. He is not flaky, flippant, or dishonest.[20]
- God's mind is filled with love, care, and compassion toward others.[21]
- The fruit of the Spirit flows from the mind of God: love, joy, peace, patience, kindness, goodness, faithfulness, gentleness, and self-control. Therefore, we are assured that His mind is peaceful, patient, and filled with care and compassion.[22]
- God's mind is confident and sure. He knows what He is capable of and is unafraid of anyone or anything.[23]
- God's mind is not rushed, compelled, or anxious but moves at a perfectly healthy rate to accomplish His works.[24]
- God's mind is full of enjoyment, certain of a glorious future, lighthearted, and soothed.[25]

If trying to figure out the mind of the Father is too lofty or elusive for us, we can look to the example of our Lord and Savior Jesus Christ. Paul said,

Have this mind among yourselves, which is yours in Christ Jesus, who, though he was in the form of God, did not count equality with God a thing to be grasped, but *emptied himself,* by *taking the form of a servant,* being born in the likeness of men. And being found in human form, he *humbled himself by becoming obedient* to the point of death, even death on a cross. (Phil. 2:5–8)

Although Paul was specifically referring to a mind-set of humility, his words are a fresh reminder that Jesus Christ lived to show us how to live. And indeed, Jesus is the beautiful example of what humanity's mind-set about life should be, with one great exception: He lived His earthly life prior to His work on the cross, and therefore His mind-set was fraught with things that the cross was going to solve. In no way am I diminishing His incredible example for us to imitate; on the contrary, I want to lift it higher with the realization that Jesus Christ was concerned with a lot of things that He was about to solve.

The Bible says that Christ was a "man of sorrows" (Isa. 53:3). We watched Him weep over Israel.[26] We saw Him cry at Lazarus's tomb.[27] Why so many tears? Part of it, I'm sure, was that His heart was broken over the sin of His people and His creation. That's still a problem. However, I believe part of His sorrow was seeing the impact of sin on His children. He took care of that at the cross. Jesus Christ is not still mourning over darkness in His people. He is not still anxious about being separated from the Father.[28] Jesus is thriving at the right hand of the Father, back where He rightfully belongs, glorified, majestic, and full of joy.

The cross changed everything.

If we're trying to think the way Jesus does now, we are to live in light of the cross and the freedom and peace that Christ provided us. We are to live in victory, authority, and power. We are to be confident that He has overcome and that we have everything we need. We are to live from a mind-set not of scarcity but of abundance. We are blessed with all the blessings of heaven.[29] The essence of our challenge is to start thinking like God does and from His perspective. We need to adopt His worldview, His version of reality.

If God is God and He built us for Him, then only His priorities, His agenda, His perception, and His reality matter. What does God say is real? He says that He is on the throne, regardless of what the world looks like. That means we must live as if God is in charge, the Master. God views the world through His victory both on the cross and in the world; therefore, we live in light of that same victory. He is the King. The two most important questions to ask in life are *What is God saying?* and *What am I going to do about it, or how am I going to align with it?*

To align with God's worldview is countercultural. It's possible but difficult. We must determine that it's the only way to live and the healthiest way to live. This world contains so many opinions about what's real and how things are supposed to be, but God alone knows. It's been that way from the beginning.[30] God has always called His people to be "set apart" (holy), to be countercultural, and to trust His Word alone.[31]

Spiritually Discerned Reality

Seeing God's perspective, appreciating His kingdom, and embracing His viewpoint is not simply a matter of intellectual assent or listening to the right facts. It is the movement and work of the Spirit in our spirits. We need God to lift the veil over our minds[32] so that we can truly see. It is God who imparts wisdom.[33] It is God who knows all things. It is God who holds truth in His pocket and who must reveal it to man.

That is why the young King Solomon (c. 1000 BC), who was selected to succeed his father, David, as the king of Israel, sought God's favor and asked for only one thing in order to run God's nation: wisdom. Solomon knew no school could teach him the ways of the Lord as thoroughly as he needed to know them. He knew if he was given all the authority of the throne without the wisdom to manage it, the nation would fall apart. Therefore, on the night God visited him in a dream and said, "Ask what I shall give you," Solomon's reply was this:

> And now, O LORD my God, you have made your servant king
> in place of David my father, although I am but a little child. I do
> not know how to go out or come in. And your servant is in the

midst of your people whom you have chosen, a great people, too many to be numbered or counted for multitude. *Give your servant therefore an understanding mind to govern your people, that I may discern between good and evil*, for who is able to govern this your great people? (1 Kings 3:7–9)

Solomon knew that wisdom was in the hands of God. He knew that as long as he was outside God's revelation, he would be guessing in the dark. Therefore, his one wish, his one request, was that God would impart to him wisdom beyond his years and experience. He wanted to know what God thought about the situations he faced. He wanted to know God's heart for his nation. He wanted to have his thoughts track with the real King's thoughts.

We need the same thing today.

That is why the Lord's brother James said, "If any of you lacks wisdom, let him ask God, who gives generously to all without reproach, and it will be given him" (James 1:5).

We need to pray and ask God for His wisdom to rule our thoughts. We need His wisdom to properly steward our lives. We need His wisdom to see what we have been built for and what purpose He intends for us. We need His wisdom to order our steps according to His will. He wants us to know it. He has been revealing truth to mankind since the dawn of creation. All we need to do is ask—oh, and pay attention to the answer.

Bare Naked

On the surface, all of this talk about us needing, needing, needing from God makes us sound desperate and weak. It would be easy to believe that God is disappointed in us and embarrassed at how foolish His created children have become. But I'm here to tell you that is not the case. God is not shocked by our ignorance. God is not alarmed by our stupidity. God is not angry at our inability. God knows everything about us. He knows our temptations, compulsions, mixed-up minds, addictions, and identity issues. Not only does He have the omniscience and the omnipresence to know the number of hairs on our heads,[34] but He has a love that compels Him to pay attention to even our thoughts, intentions, and motivations.[35] He created us. He knows things about us that we will never know. He sustains us, which means that every day He observes what we lack. He empowers us, and He even knows the words we are going to say before they appear on our tongues.[36]

The Bible speaks of what I call a "Theo-echocardiogram." *Theo* means God, and an echocardiogram is a sonogram reading of our hearts. In other words, God tests our hearts.

> I the LORD *search the heart and test the mind*, to give every man according to his ways, according to the fruit of his deeds. (Jer. 17:10)[37]

> And you shall remember the whole way that the LORD your God has led you these forty years in the wilderness, that he might humble you, *testing you to know what was in your heart*, whether you would keep his commandments or not. (Deut. 8:2)[38]

God knows what He's working with.[39] We have to stop the silliness of trying to hide things from God.[40] We have to stop believing the Enemy's lies that God is shocked by what He sees in us. We have to stop thinking that our inadequacy changes our relationship to the Lord.

He made us. He knows what we're like.

God has always compensated for our helplessness, our frailty, our feebleness, and our wimpiness.[41] He has never worked with any other type of human. You and I are not the first on the assembly line to appear defective. I internally chuckle when I hear people confess their inabilities to God as though He would be surprised by it. The truth is that we've never been anything other than unable. It's not an insult; it's just reality.

God knows that if there's going to be anything of value at the table, He has to bring it. He knows that if we have any shot of living the life that He wants us to live, He will be the one to initiate it, sustain it, direct it, and empower it. He knows that it's in our fallen nature to deviate. He knows that it's our fleshly appetite to sin. He knows that we are selfish and rebellious. He knows that we are clueless as to what really matters in this world and how things actually work in our universe.

He knows.

He's our only chance to get it right.

How He Works

God is not as interested in our getting things right as He is in our getting out of the way and allowing Him to make things right. We need to let Him do what He does best: make things the way He likes them. The Holy Spirit is continually working in us and through us to align with the will of the Father. God is more concerned with our spiritual and emotional health than we are. Remember, the condition of the sheep reflects more on the aptitude of the shepherd than on the behavior of the sheep.

When God takes territory for our freedom, we stand on it and don't let it go.[42]

When God restores a relationship, we fight to maintain that unity.[43]

When God brings peace, we hold on tight in faith and hide behind the shield He has given us.[44]

When God restores our minds, we use that clarity to follow Him.[45]

When God defeats the Enemy and kicks him out, we don't open the door and invite him back in.[46]

When God brings us wise counsel and instruction, we pay attention and implement it.[47]

When God opens His Word to us, we read it, meditate on it, and apply it.[48]

When God shows us who we are, we remember our identity and live as His children.

The process of our sanctification —becoming more like Christ— does not involve God waiting while we try to get our stuff together. It is a process by which the Holy Spirit shapes us into the image of Christ. God wants us to look like Him and to cut away anything in us that's not like Him. We don't have to wait for heaven to be glorified (although that will be the culmination); the Lord is able to emerge in us for His glory from the moment of conversion.[49] The very essence of honoring our Lord and King is to allow Him to have His way in us.

Will we let Him do what He wants to do in order for Him to be praised?

Chapter 10

Replacement Therapy

Seventy-three million light-years from us is a *supermassive* black hole. It's 660 million times larger than our sun, with a cloud of gas circling it at approximately one million miles per hour, and it's swallowing huge planetary objects.

Should we be worried?

No. We have a smaller—but still massive—black hole much closer to us, at the center of our own Milky Way galaxy, and it hasn't sucked us in yet. Truthfully, black holes aren't cosmic vacuum cleaners trying to gobble up the rest of the universe.[1] Nevertheless, these incredible phenomena have such an extraordinary gravitational pull due to their density that if something comes too near them, it will be sucked in and lost forever. A black hole may not be a vacuum cleaner, but it sure is a sucker.

A black hole seems to be what remains after a massive star dies. Allow me to share a brief science lesson: Stars are made of gases held together by a central gravitational force. They are a delicate balance of exploding (outward) force and gravitational (inward) force. As a star uses up its matter, it condenses it so tightly that it heats up to a detonation called a supernova, spewing out most of its contents.

But at the very core, the gravitational pull remains and pulls in on itself, creating a black hole—a void, a place of darkness that continues pulling anything around it inside.

Voids must be filled. Until they are filled, they continue sucking things into them. God seems to have created a need for all objects in this universe to be filled with something, anything, and that is true of our hearts, minds, and souls. They are ever-craving to be filled, so if something is removed, they will demand a replacement. If the replacement isn't healthy, it won't be enough, and they will keep grabbing the closest fillers they can find.

Paul taught this concept in 1 Corinthians:

> Now concerning the matters about which you wrote: "It is good for a man not to have sexual relations with a woman." *But because of the temptation to sexual immorality, each man should have his own wife and each woman her own husband.* The husband should give to his wife her conjugal rights, and likewise the wife to her husband. For the wife does not have authority over her own body, but the husband does. Likewise the husband does not have authority over his own body, but the wife does. *Do not deprive one another, except perhaps by agreement for a limited time, that you may devote yourselves to prayer; but then come together again, so that Satan may not tempt you because of your lack of self-control.* (1 Cor. 7:1–5)

In essence, what Paul expressed in this teaching on sexual design within a marriage is that when there is a strong pull (libido) that is not fed with something healthy (appropriate sexual contact), the void it creates (abstinence) leaves room for unhealthy elements (satanic temptation for unhealthy sexual fulfillment) to fill that space. In other words, if we don't manage wisely our desires and fill them with healthy things, unhealthy things may take their place.

Voids fill themselves. Just a glance at human nature reveals this to be true. There is the young woman with an absent dad who has never been single a day in her adult life but flits to one relationship after another. There is the compulsive marijuana smoker whose emotional hurt and disappointment with life drive him to numb his feelings and escape from his problems. There is the young man searching for significance who works so hard that he has no time for health, life, relationship, joy, or God. If there is a void in our lives, we will fill it.

This is where the church has historically gotten it wrong. Too many sermons are filled with instruction on how we need to remove things from our lives. I may be guilty of this as a pastor myself. We preach series after series about taking off the old self,[2] rooting out the sin, crucifying the flesh, and turning from our wicked ways, but we never spend the appropriate time talking about what to replace them with. As modern-day Christians, we are very clear about what we are against but not quite sure what we are for. If we do know, we certainly aren't talking about it enough.

Christianity cannot simply be "sin management" or a struggle to stop doing things. Christianity needs to be a thriving relationship with God filled with the Holy Spirit and all the incredible blessings He has given us. We need to be so filled up that the Holy Spirit forces out the evil.

If a glass of water contained a pinch or so of dirt, how would we clean it out? Would we spend our energy trying to remove the granules with tweezers, or would we run the glass under the faucet of clean, fresh water and force out the dirty water? I argue that Christianity needs to be a lot more about what we put in our lives than what we take out. A vessel filled to the brim with the Holy Spirit leaves little room for the kingdom of darkness. Jesus said that the Holy Spirit gives us "living water."[3] Instead of describing animate liquid, He was using the metaphor for running water, ever-filling water, like a spring out of the ground flowing continually. As the Holy Spirit pours into us, He should naturally cleanse our hearts without us becoming obsessed with simple removal.

We were never designed to be voids.

Notice the progression of holy living mentioned in the book of Colossians:

> *Since, then,* you have been raised with Christ, *set your hearts on things above,* where Christ is, seated at the right hand of God. *Set your minds on things above,* not on earthly things. . . . *Put to death, therefore, whatever belongs to your earthly nature:* sexual immorality, impurity, lust, evil desires and greed, which is idolatry. Because of these, the wrath of God is coming. You used to walk in these ways, in the life you once lived. But *now you must rid yourselves of all such things as these*: anger, rage, malice, slander, and filthy language from your lips. Do not lie to each other, since *you have taken off your old self with its practices and have put on the new self, which is being renewed in knowledge in the image of its Creator.* . . . *Therefore, as God's chosen people,* holy and dearly loved, *clothe yourselves with compassion, kindness, humility, gentleness and patience. Bear with each other* and forgive one another if any of you has a grievance against someone. *Forgive* as the Lord forgave you. And over all these virtues *put on love,* which binds them all together in perfect unity. (3:1–14 NIV)[4]

Paul begins with our new identities. He says that we have been raised with Christ, which means we are a new creation, born again with all the sin of our lives dead and gone. We are alive and free. Then he tells us what to focus on in order to live into the potential of our new lives: heavenly, good, healthy, life-giving thoughts. He goes on to tell us that some behaviors do not align with our new identities—things like selfishness, lashing out at others in anger, and wicked thoughts. We need to let go of these, and when the cravings come up, we must ignore them and treat them as though they're dead to us. He says that since we have put on our new selves, we need to live appropriately and be aligned with our new identities. The thoughts and actions consistent with our new, healthy nature are things like humility, kindness, and patience. We take off what's old and sinful, and we put on what's new and good.

Clearly, I'm not saying that we don't need to stop certain behaviors or root out the garbage. I'm merely saying that when we let go of things that are no longer aligned with our new nature, that have been revealed by the Lord to be sinful, or that we no longer need, then we must refill our hearts with the great things of God and the blessings that flow from His throne. Our identity shift (from orphan to child of God) comes first, and it's followed by the shift of lifestyle (from bondage to freedom). Too many times we try to reverse the process and begin with trying to force new, good behaviors without the proper mind-set in place to keep them healthy and pure. If we are merely moral on the outside but retain the same identities and thought processes on the inside, our changes will not last. Transformation always begins in our thoughts.

With every removal of the bad, we backfill with the good. It's not appropriate to go on a massive removal mission without keeping our eyes on what we are replacing it with. That will only backfire. A hole in a boat needs to be patched, or we will forever be scooping out the same water that keeps coming in. If there are multiple holes in the hull, we don't wait to scoop out all the water before we plug them. We plug them first.

The Refilling Station

We secure our minds by backfilling with good.

We anchor ourselves firmly in our new identity in Christ

and allow the Holy Spirit to point out the various areas of sin in His timing, with His wisdom, and prepped with His power. As each area is removed, we fill ourselves with healthy, life-giving elements.

For example, let's say the Holy Spirit highlights as unhealthy your need to be at the corner bar every night after work. He shows you that you are going there to be noticed, to be accepted, and to periodically make terrible choices due to your distorted cravings. You agree with Him and decide to change your behavior. But instead of deciding to sit alone at home each night, staring at the wall and wishing you were at the bar, a smarter choice would be to plan something else fun on most of those nights. Maybe instead of going to the bar, you have a group of friends over for hot wings and football. Maybe you focus on developing one or two meaningful connections instead of a barrage of unhealthy acquaintances. Maybe a softball league is one step closer to redirecting your time to something that's healthy.

It's one step, one decision at a time.

Too often the term "slippery slope" is used for bad stuff. Usually, it means that if we make one bad choice, it's going to be that much easier to make another bad choice. Before we know it, we have backslid down the slippery hill. But why can't it work for the good decisions too? Is the good hill not slippery enough? I think that every good decision makes the next one easier. I think that we underestimate the influence of good, shortchanging the freedom and power that God has given us to change. Not only is change for the better possible; it's probable.

What Repentance Really Means

Repentance is a powerful and complex word. It's used all over the New Testament to talk about how we need to deal with sin. Jesus used it. Paul used it. Unfortunately, most of us have been told only one part of what repentance really means. When we hear that word, we think, "be super sorry for what you've done and promise to never do it again."[5] Most repentance sermons use the common illustration of a U-turn, explaining accurately that repenting means to turn around and go the opposite direction.[6] Unfortunately, to describe only what we're turning from leaves out the positive side of the equation—what we are turning to. It's not just about stopping one way of thinking but about replacing that thinking with a godly perspective.

When Jesus told His listeners to "repent, for the kingdom of heaven is at hand" (Matt. 3:2), He did not simply mean "feel terrible for your wickedness now that I'm here." He meant much more than that, and, in fact, I believe He was focused primarily on the positive side of that word. *Repent* doesn't only mean to turn away but to change one's mind and start agreeing with God.[7] Jesus meant that upon His arrival, everything needed to change. Mankind was now engaging with God up close. God's rule was now present. Both wickedness and righteousness were coming to light. The Enemy was being pushed back. Victory was overcoming sin, and there was a new way to look at life.

The kind of repentance that involves changed behavior goes deeper than mere regret. It is rooted in our thoughts. The gospel author Mark quoted Jesus as saying, "The time is fulfilled, and the kingdom of God is at hand; *repent and believe in the gospel*" (Mark 1:15). There is no repentance without belief, no leaving without joining, no avoidance without engagement, no rejection without acceptance.

It's not a new concept. God spoke through Isaiah as well: "Let the wicked *forsake his way*, and the unrighteous man *his thoughts; let him return to the* LORD, that he may have compassion on him, and to our God, for he will abundantly pardon" (Isa. 55:7).[8]

Repent and believe. It's all part of the same process, two sides of the same coin.

A Renewed Mind

This brings us back to the premise of this whole book: our thoughts affect our actions. As a man thinks and believes, so also will he live. The world does not sin and therefore become wicked, but because of wickedness the world sins.[9] As Christians, we don't sin because we don't love God; we sin because we don't fully understand and embrace our new identities and callings in the Lord. We not only need to know why something needs to be done; we also need to emotionally agree with it deep down. We don't just need accurate information; we also need our hearts to believe it. The disconnect from our brains to our minds and hearts is both emotional and spiritual.

When the Bible talks about needing a renewed mind—"Do not be conformed to this world, but *be transformed by the renewal of your mind*, that by testing you may discern what is the will of God, what is good and acceptable and perfect" (Rom. 12:2)[10]—it's not speaking about simply hearing the truth. Billions of people throughout history have heard truth, and it made no impact on them. Instead, renewal implies that there is a process by which the truth is heard, listened to, considered, embraced, and put into practice. Renewal begins with a determination to receive[11] and a heart that is open to transformation.

Having a renewed mind certainly begins with our need to focus on the Lord ferociously and keep our minds stayed on Him. It is not merely a matter of believing our identity, as if that is a passive procedure. There is a great discipline involved. We are leaky vessels—cracked pots, if you will. We can have the truth in us, yet it can seep out and be replaced by lies in no time. We can receive the Word, yet over time it gets choked out by the cares of life.[12] Jesus lived the victorious life in the flesh that He did because of His disciplined lifestyle of abiding with the Father. We are called to do the same thing.

There is tremendous benefit to what some call the "spiritual disciplines"—things we remove from or add into our lives for the purpose of training our bodies and minds. They are practices like silence, solitude, fasting, community, secrecy, chastity, rejoicing, and thanksgiving. Perhaps the late, brilliant Dallas Willard did the greatest writing on this subject.[13] I don't want to pretend to be in his league, and I don't have the time to discuss the topic fully, but it's important to note that the spiritual disciplines are just as much about what to add to life as what to remove. Both involve a decision and determination to live like Christ so that we might have victory as He did.

So what was Christ's lifestyle like? What did His "every day" consist of? What patterns of living would we see if we spied on the Son of God during His days on earth? Although we could speculate, the Bible shares a few rhythms of life that reveal the various spiritual disciplines Jesus employed. For example, we have already extensively studied His use of fasting in the desert temptation at the beginning of His ministry. He fasted in order to deny His flesh and discipline His cravings so He could submit to the Father's will.[14] Luke 5:16 tells us that "Jesus often withdrew to lonely places and prayed" (NIV), utilizing the disciplines of silence and solitude in order to hear the direction of the Father.[15] Clearly, the responses to Satan in the desert reflect Christ's discipline of Scripture memorization. Jesus taught the discipline of secrecy verbally in the Sermon on the Mount.[16] The Garden of Gethsemane and the cross were obvious demonstrations of the discipline of sacrifice. And, although Jesus didn't need to engage in the discipline of confession, He clearly used the discipline of prayer continually.[17] It was

Christ's mind-set that led to His lifestyle, which led to the results of His extraordinary life.

Kenneth Boa shared the heart of Dallas Willard when he said,

> We have bought the illusion that we can be like Christ without imitating his spirituality. If we wish to be like our Master, we must imitate his practice . . . To ask the question What would Jesus do? without practicing the habits we know he practiced is to attempt to run a marathon without prior training. . . . We desire to know Christ more deeply, but we shun the lifestyle that would make it happen . . . There is no shortcut to spiritual formation. [18]

In this same vein I want to cite one more beautiful instruction from the apostle Paul: "Finally, brothers, whatever is true, whatever is honorable, whatever is just, whatever is pure, whatever is lovely, whatever is commendable, if there is any excellence, if there is anything worthy of praise, think about these things" (Phil. 4:8).

When our minds are focused solely on things that are earthly, mundane, everyday, troubled, anxious, fearful, sad, depressing, limited, weak, or distracting, we cannot keep perspective on who we really are in Christ. The Bible tells us that we are seated with Christ in the heavenly realm,[19] that our citizenship is there,[20] and that we draw resources, strength, guidance, and health from there.[21] It's not enough to try not to dwell on things of this world; we must fill our minds with thoughts from heaven.

The Holy Spirit wants to run His expansion project from the inside out. The more we fill our minds and hearts with truth from the mouth of God, the more we will agree with the direction of the Holy Spirit, and the more we will force out the average and cling to the divine. We use our God-enabled self-control to restrict what's not of God, and we determine to allow God the freedom to renew what is of Him.

When our minds are locked in to the Lord, incredible things can happen. Our reality changes.

You keep him in *perfect peace* whose mind is stayed on you, because he trusts in you. (Isa. 26:3)

Do not be anxious about anything, but in everything by prayer and supplication with thanksgiving let your requests be made known to God. And *the peace of God, which surpasses all understanding, will guard your hearts and your minds in Christ Jesus.* (Phil. 4:6–7)

When our minds are on the Lord and we think about His power, His sovereignty, and His control, our fear of our surroundings and circumstances begins to pale in comparison. The result is that peace enters our minds and hearts, because we know that someone far more capable is on the job of our protection and well-being. We began anxious, with our bodies reacting to the stress of the anxiety, but with a change of mind-set into faith and trust in the Lord, our bodies begin to relax and be comforted.

The circumstances remained the same. The problems were still there. The enemies were still lurking. But when the thoughts shifted from trouble to safety, the reality shifted in concert from fear to peace. It was not merely a change in perceived reality but actual reality.

Maybe the most shocking example of a person's reality changing because of his focus on Jesus is Peter on the Sea of Galilee. The disciples were out on the lake at night when Jesus came walking toward them on the surface of the water. While others cowered in fear, Peter called out to Jesus—who invited the impulsive follower to join Him. Peter had spent his life as a fisherman, so he knew all about water. He knew that boats float and people sink, and in his old reality he wouldn't have lasted a second on that water. Yet despite all that, Peter set aside his doubts and fear and replaced them with a laser-like focus on Christ. He stepped out of the boat—and walked on water. Yet as amazing as this was, it didn't last long. Scripture also says, "When he saw the wind, he was afraid, and beginning to sink he cried out, 'Lord, save me'" (Matt. 14:30). The difference between walking on water and sinking was a mind firmly fixed on Jesus.

When we see things like God sees things, when we trust Him more than we trust ourselves, when we walk by faith and not by sight,[22] we live differently. Our world changes.

We need a different worldview. So how do we get it?

Soul Talk

I have written some in this book and extensively in my prior book, *How to Live in Fear*, about the power of God's Word and how it renews our mind, changes our thoughts, and flips our reality. I have honored the critical aspects of prayer and deep intimacy with God. I have explained that worship is a key not only to praising the King but to getting our eyes on the most important thing while God fights our battles. Therefore, having covered the most vital tools for developing a different worldview, I want to turn our attention back to ourselves for a moment and talk about proper stewardship of our souls.

King David talked to himself, and I'm so thankful he did. While some would have observed it and tried to offer him meds, the spiritually attuned simply thanked him. We wouldn't have the majority of Psalms if he hadn't. He didn't just journal; he spoke out loud to himself. He talked directly to his soul.

> *Why are you cast down, O my soul,*
>> and why are you in turmoil within me?
> *Hope in God;* for I shall again praise him,
>> my salvation and my God. (Ps. 42:5–6)[23]

> *Bless the LORD, O my soul,*
>> and all that is within me,
>> bless his holy name!
> *Bless the LORD, O my soul,*
>> *and forget not all his benefits,*
> who forgives all your iniquity,
>> who heals all your diseases,
> who redeems your life from the pit,
>> who crowns you with steadfast love and mercy,
> who satisfies you with good
>> so that your youth is renewed like the
>>> eagle's. (Ps. 103:1–5)[24]

> *Return, O my soul, to your rest;*
>> for the LORD has dealt bountifully with you. (Ps. 116:7)

> O LORD, my heart is not lifted up;
>> my eyes are not raised too high;
> I do not occupy myself with things
>> too great and too marvelous for me.
> But *I have calmed and quieted my soul,*
>> *like a weaned child with its mother;*
>> like a weaned child is my soul within me. (Ps. 131:1–2)

David talked to his soul. When he told it to change how it was thinking, he was speaking truth to himself. He was convincing himself of what was right and true. First he saw the condition of his soul and called it out; then he told his heart what to do. He replaced his old way of thinking with a new way, his mind-set of fear and complaining with one of praise and truth.

David determined to look at reality and not just his emotional perspective. He was a good steward of his mind, will, and emotions, and a good manager of his body. He was taking back control from his feelings. Feelings are good, but if they are not shaped, molded, and harnessed, they begin to betray themselves. I am not a fan of logic-only Christianity that says no emotions are to be trusted. Emotions are part of how God made us, and we are to direct them, not quash them. But if left alone and unruly, they will begin to wreck the very purpose they were designed for by God. David knew this and began to tell himself how things needed to be.

He wasn't the only one who did this.

Jeremiah did it:

> Remember my affliction and my wanderings, the wormwood and the gall! My soul continually remembers it and is bowed down within me. But this I call to mind, and therefore I have hope: The steadfast love of the LORD never ceases; his mercies never come to an end; they are new every morning; great is your faithfulness. "The LORD is my portion," says my soul, "therefore I will hope in him." The LORD is good to those who wait for him, to the soul who seeks him. It is good that one should wait quietly for the salvation of the LORD. (Lam. 3:19–26)

And Nehemiah did it: "I was very angry when I heard their outcry and these words. *I took counsel with myself*, and I brought charges against the nobles and the officials" (Neh. 5:6–7).

These men knew the power of speaking truth to themselves. Unfortunately, not all soul talk is healthy.

I'm sure it's not difficult for any of us to recall times when we have allowed our minds to go places and say things about ourselves that aren't true. In fact, I would suggest that most of our soul talk, most of our self-talk, most of our thinking isn't healthy at all.

That is why it is so crucial that we speak to ourselves in a life-giving manner.[25] We must remain fixed on what is right and true.[26] When the Bible talks about meditating on God's law day and night,[27] it doesn't mean keeping the rules in front of us as much as keeping the truth and reality of God in front of us. I'm not talking about the power of positive thinking or delving into the confusing world of vows and curses; I'm talking about consistently maintaining control of our thoughts by reminding ourselves of what is true. Some of us in the church have abandoned the idea of self talk as a product of misguided psychology of the 1970s, but I think that is foolish. I believe that we need to redeem the concept, recenter it upon God's Word, and allow the Holy Spirit to use it to guide and direct us.

Let me leave you for now with a challenge: imagine awesome.

It's so easy to imagine bad stuff, scary outcomes, and failure around the corner. Why not imagine what could happen that would be great? What if we lived truly free as Christ died for us to be?[28] What if we replaced our faulty mind-sets with truthful ones? What if we had the peace that passed all understanding that would guard our hearts and minds, like the Bible says?[29] What if we were truly mature and complete in Him?[30] What if we walked in the confidence, authority, and power that Jesus walked this earth with? What if we exercised our faith with firm determination, believing that not only was Christ coming again, but that our future was gloriously fixed in heaven?

What if we were healthy?

What if our thoughts aligned with His?

What if our doubts, regrets, shame, and insecurities were left at the foot of the cross?

What if we could think like we want to think and not have all the irritating hang-ups that wreck our days?

What if we were secure enough in our identities that it would take far more than one rude comment to derail us?

What if we cared less about what others thought and more about what God thought?

What if we could love other people instead of being scared of them or wanting to use them as consumables for our insatiable egos?

What if we truly believed that everywhere we set our feet was owned by our Father and therefore safe for us to tread?

What if money wasn't the driving factor for our daily decisions, but God's will was?

What if we were able to live at the Holy Spirit's pace and not just run breathlessly into tomorrow?

What if God had more for us?

What if tomorrow God was waiting to bless us again?

What if we were filled with more spiritual gifts than we anticipated?

What if . . . ?

Chapter 11

Who's the Boss?

E nough is enough.
We are not victims.

So many conversations in church or at the coffee shop center on our problems and how everything is so difficult. Whether it's couched as a prayer request or is simply banter on social media, we share our frustrations and disappointments far more than we do our blessings. Ironically, many of us only read the portions of the Bible that reinforce our "woe is me" condition. We love the camaraderie of Paul's wrestling with the flesh in Romans 7:

> For *I do not understand my own actions*. For *I do not do what I want, but I do the very thing I hate*. . . . For I have the desire to do what is right, but *not the ability to carry it out*. For I do not do the good I want, *but the evil I do not want is what I keep on doing*. . . . *making me captive to the law of sin that dwells in my members. Wretched man that I am!* Who will deliver me from this body of death? (vv. 15–24)

But we forget verse 25: "Thanks be to God through Jesus Christ our Lord!"

It's true—there's a wrestling match, there's a war in our bodies and spirits, and yes, it's hard. But we are not alone in this, and we are not doomed to failure! Jesus Christ is the One who can set us free, not just when we get to heaven, but increasingly so right here on earth.

Paul was not done with his treatise on war against the flesh and sin in Romans 7. He went on in chapter 8 to talk about victory that we can have in Jesus by the power of the Holy Spirit. He stated blatantly, "No, in all these things we are more than conquerors through him who loved us" (Rom. 8:37).

Although the specific context of verse 37 is more about persecutions, it's still applicable to our discussion here. We are more than conquerors. Jesus Christ died for our sins and set us free from the law of sin and death. This means that nothing stands against us today that we cannot overcome. The Lord has provided a way to lead us to freedom.

We are not victims.

It's time to get mad. It's time to hold Satan accountable for all the chaos he has inflicted upon this world by introducing sin and death and deceiving us about who we are and what is true. It's time to get angry at all the time we have wasted by falling prey to our own passions, lusts, cravings, addictions, implosions, desires, dysfunction, and poor decisions. We must determine that we will not be pushed around any longer. After all, who's the boss here? Universally, it's God as our King; locally, it's us.

It's time to buckle down, control our thoughts, and bring them under submission. When Paul the apostle talked about taking control of our lives, he said it like this:

> Do you not know that in a race all the runners run, but only one receives the prize? So run that you may obtain it. *Every athlete exercises self-control* in all things. They do it to receive

a perishable wreath, but we an imperishable. So *I do not run aimlessly*; I do not box as one beating the air. But *I discipline my body and keep it under control*, lest after preaching to others I myself should be disqualified. (1 Cor. 9:24–27)

Let me remind us that every time there is a command in Scripture, it serves as an encouragement, because if God told us to do it, He will provide the power and ability! Therefore, Paul's call to discipline is a promise that we have the ability and authority to discipline and train our bodies and minds: we get to decide what goes in our heads, determine what we focus on, choose where we go and what we do. If our minds want to launch back into a pattern of dysfunction, we have the right to stop them and choose to react a different way. If our anger rises up and starts to overwhelm us, we have the leverage to refuse its invasion and redirect it in a healthy manner. We decide what goes on within the territory of our minds!

This is the time and place for righteous anger. We are victors, conquerors. We are the ones who tell our minds what to think about, tell our souls what to dwell on, tell our hearts what to long for, and tell our bodies what they can and can't do. We are in charge. I don't want to waste any more time and energy on things that hurt me. I'm sick and tired of worrying about things that will never happen. I'm tired of stressing about things I shouldn't stress about. I'm frustrated by all the anxiety I carry for things I have no control over. I'm tired of forgetting that I am God's child, not a permanent resident of this world. I'm irritated at believing lies and thinking that my identity rests in what I do. It's time to fight back.

From the Football Field to Our Heads

All high-level athletes train both their bodies and their minds. Mental toughness can make or break a game. When you are down

42–28 in the fourth quarter, it's tempting to give up. When you are ahead by that much, it's hard to remain motivated and close the game. But it's the mentally strong and disciplined athletes who finish the job and refuse to let their emotions push them around. They harness the passion, they feel the intensity, they live off the rush—and when it's go-time, they take control.

Lots of sports talk shows praise a team's "swagger," and the untrained Christian ear may be offended at the highlighting of what looks like pride. But it's not pride; it's confidence. It's the certainty that the team can get the job done. It's rising above the victim mentality into one of a victor. It's dwelling in the space of abundance rather than scarcity. It's knowing that they have the talent, and they put in the work to use all of that talent out on the field. Whatever comes their way, they already believe they can defeat it.

We need a little more swagger on the battlefield of our minds. Of course, swagger looks stupid on an ill-equipped and unprepared team, but we have everything we need.

Managers

God created the world, made a place called Eden, and planted a special garden there. He knew how it should be watered, how it should be tended, how it should be cared for. God took great pleasure in His creation of said garden—and then He took His prized possession and put it in the hands of Adam and Eve so they could manage it for Him.[1] Adam and Eve didn't own it; they were simply managers. They were tasked with the responsibility of its care without having full ownership.

Jesus said that God's kingdom here on earth was handled the same way.[2] God set up a plan to bless the world. He created a people group, the Jews, to be His hands, feet, light, and voice. He endowed them with a special attention, a special authority, a special protection, and a special power. He set them into a special place with special leadership. He gave them everything they needed to manage His stuff. They weren't owners; they were managers.

We are managers of our minds. We aren't owners of them, as we saw in chapter 9. God owns them; we don't. God will hold us accountable for how we manage our minds and handle our hearts. He has given us everything we need to manage them well. It's time to get to managing!

Getting Down to Business

I want to share six practical and basic steps to start the process of gaining mental toughness and a victor mentality:

1. **Agree with God.** We need to agree with God that He is the boss and that we take our cues from Him. We need to determine that His way is best and trust His renovation project. We need to tune our ears toward the voice of the Holy Spirit and put into practice what God says in His Word. We need to repent from double-mindedness, as James says;[3] clean things up; and draw near to God so that He can show us the way to freedom.

2. **Stop making it worse.** We may not be able to take out all the garbage ourselves, but we can certainly stop stockpiling it. As much as we are able, we need to stop the terrible inputs and the in-flow of dysfunctional ideas. We need to move away from toxicity, both in our mind-sets and in others, in order to get some space to undertake the cleaning process relatively free from distraction.[4] Remember, our thoughts can only grab from the library that we stocked. The images, thoughts, ideas, drives, and desires we allowed in initially or even fostered by habitual pattern are stored in our mind.

Although they seem to pop up at random, they are actually coming from a storehouse we loaded. The more books we clean out and the more new, healthy volumes we replace them with, the fewer options the Enemy has to utilize in temptation and distraction.

3. **Simplify.** Our minds are messy. We cannot handle everything in one day, and we don't need to set expectations of conquering the promised land in an afternoon. We need to slow down, shut off the pollution valve, and just sit with God for a time. We need to focus on the basics: Who is He? Who are we in light of who He is? What are we supposed to do in light of all that?

The simple believes everything, but *the prudent gives thought to his steps.* (Prov. 14:15)

4. **Train rightly.** Remember, transformation is not a matter of trying harder but training smarter. What we cannot do today we may be able to do tomorrow, if we are willing to train right. The more we soak in the Lord and take advantage of the spiritual disciplines He modeled for us, the more control we will have to adjust what's out of alignment in our heads. It's about purposeful living and individual good choices, day after day. We need to live on purpose, not in reaction. We, not our circumstances, set the tone. We are called to deny ourselves that which doesn't help us grow and pursue that which does.

Spiritual disciplines expert Dallas Willard taught us to say no to the things that you can, so you can learn to say no to the things that you can't.[5] Paul the apostle said, "When I was a child, I spoke like a child, *I thought like a child,* I reasoned like a child. *When I became a man, I gave up childish ways*" (1 Cor. 13:11). Peter said, "Therefore, *preparing your minds for action*, and being *sober-minded*, set your hope fully on the grace that will be brought to you at the revelation of Jesus Christ" (1 Peter 1:13).

5. **Take thoughts captive.** Once we gain some control over our minds through proper training, it's time to put that control to use. When we detect a dysfunctional mind-set, an improper view of identity, a sinful instinct, or a wayward thought, it's time to grab hold of it and submit it to God. The only reason our distorted thoughts have so much power is that we have empowered them through patterns of agreement (habits) all these years. Old, wicked, and dysfunctional thoughts are not inherently more powerful than our new healthy thoughts; it's simply a matter of what we use more often. But make no mistake, we have the power to change them. Paul, our biblical mind-control tour guide, said it like this: "For the weapons of our warfare are not of the flesh but have *divine power to destroy strongholds. We destroy arguments and every lofty opinion raised against the knowledge of God, and take every thought captive to obey Christ*, being ready to punish every disobedience, when your obedience is complete" (2 Cor. 10:4-6).

6. **Walk in freedom.** Keeping in step with the Holy Spirit is a constant decision. We need to make good choices consciously until they become instinctive. We need to say yes to the Lord, however hard it may be up front, until doing otherwise seems foreign. We need to cling to our identity in Christ and live as though it is so, despite our circumstances. Walking in freedom is difficult but not impossible. It begins with one good choice, founded on a solid identity, followed by another good choice—and so on.

Redeemed Time, Minds, and Lives

Is it too late for us? Have we lived one way for too long so that now it's impossible to turn the ship around? Are our minds so entrenched in bad thinking that we can never recover?

Absolutely not.

Have we wasted time and wasted aspects of our lives? Yes. But Jesus is really good at making up for lost time, and He's incredible at redeeming lives. He can even make gold out of the garbage of your past. He can take bad mistakes and turn them into divine realities. (Consider that Messiah Jesus came from the line of Solomon, the product of David's relationship with Bathsheba, which began with infidelity and the murder of her first husband, a great man.)

Paul wrote in Romans 8,

> Likewise *the Spirit helps us in our weakness.* For *we do not know* what to pray for as we ought, but *the Spirit himself intercedes for us* with groanings too deep for words. And he who searches hearts knows what is the mind of the Spirit, because *the Spirit intercedes for the saints* according to the will of God. And we know that *for those who love God all things work together for good, for those who are called according to his purpose.* (vv. 26–28)

Paul isn't saying that all things are good. It's not that we simply need to look at them through a different lens. Some things *are* bad, and some mistakes really mess us up. We can do some extraordinary damage. The Bible doesn't disagree. But God is bigger than our failures, larger than our problems, and more magnificent than our weaknesses. Although we have bad thinking patterns, although we have hurt many people, although we have created terrible habits, that is not the end of the story. God knows how to take all of that dirt and form a man and woman out of it, breathe His very own breath into them, and make them live once again.

Tough Love from a Cave and the Desert

In 1 Kings 18 we read one of the boldest showdowns of faith in all of history. First the prophet Elijah went head to head with the 450 idolatrous prophets of Baal and called down fire from heaven. As if that wasn't enough, he prayed for rain after a three-year drought (which was started by his prayers),[6] and God answered him, showering the land with liquid life. But in chapter 19 Elijah found out that the evil king and queen of Israel wanted his head for killing their prophets and embarrassing them publicly. Elijah ran for his life and, after collapsing from exhaustion, received a supernatural heavenly meal from an angel that sustained him for forty days. How sweet and tender was God to him?

Elijah found himself in a cave, overcome with depression and hopelessness. Instead of being fired up, confident, and thankful for God's world-class miracles and miraculous provision, Elijah was consumed with the notion that he was the only prophet of Yahweh left and was merely delaying his inevitable murder at the hands of Queen Jezebel. In that moment, God called out to him and asked one simple question: "What are you doing here, Elijah?" (1 Kings 19:9). Elijah poured out his complaining and fearful heart and told God his problems. In response, God told him to go to the mouth of the cave to stand before Him.

Elijah emerged from the cave with his cloak wrapped around him, probably with a dour face and tearstained cheeks. God put on an extraordinary display of supernatural phenomenon: hurricane-force winds, earthquake, and fire. Yet God did not speak in any of the three. It was not until after the last flash of flame that God whispered in a still, small voice. We can imagine Elijah quieting his heart and straining to hear the voice of God, longing to hear the comforting words of the Father. And God said, "What are you doing here, Elijah?"

Apparently, God didn't hear Elijah the first time—or perhaps during the fireworks show Gabriel interrupted the Lord and distracted Him, causing Him to forget the conversation He'd had just a little while ago. So Elijah, ever the patient prophet with the Lord (insert sarcasm here), decided to pour out his grumblings and complaints once again: "I've been all-in for You, God; all of Israel has turned against You in rebellion, but not me. The bad guys have killed all of Your prophets and wrecked all Your worship stuff. And now they're going to come for me."

What did the Lord say? What comfort did He give? What did His understanding nature reveal?

In essence, God said, "I've got some jobs for you. Go to Syria and anoint a new king there, and do the same in Israel. On the way I need you to hand off to your replacement prophet, a young man named Elisha who can get the job done. Oh, and by the way, I have seven thousand other prophets like you who haven't caved to the pressure."

Not exactly the Hallmark-card encouragement of the century. In fact, God could have stopped at His first two questions: "What are you doing here?" They seem to suggest that Elijah had no business being shut up in a cave, feeling sorry for himself, when he had a job to do. Not only did God not let him off the hook, but He added in new responsibilities and ordered His replacement. Why? Why didn't God go soft on him? Why didn't God soothe his heart and affirm his depression?

Because it wasn't appropriate.

God knew Elijah's true condition. He knew what Elijah didn't know. He knew that although Elijah felt beaten, he wasn't. He knew that although Elijah felt hopeless, he wasn't. He knew that Elijah was listening to the world—which was telling him he was in danger with no protection. He was listening to the flesh—which was saying that he was a lone voice in a world of evil. He was listening to the Devil—who told him that God didn't really care about him and wasn't really in charge. God knew the truth: Elijah was focused on wrong perspectives. God had more strength to give Elijah, more resources, more hope, more fire, more power, more encouragement that he didn't know about. God is not going to affirm something that isn't true.

Do you know what *enabling* means?

Although enabling technically means "helping to accomplish something," the term is used in a negative way in the psychology world to describe affirming something in someone that isn't healthy, and by our words or actions encouraging that poor behavior. God will not enable His people in dysfunctional thinking. He will not make it easier for us to give up hope, be lost in fear, be overwhelmed by problems, or feel abandoned. He brings life. He brings hope. He brings solutions. Although He may allow challenge and trial and pain and fear to come, He will not encourage His children to embrace them or be absorbed by them. God has no problem pouring down the rain and flooding the earth as long as He has prepared us to build the ark in advance, but He will not fill up the boat to sink it. Remember, it's the water on the inside of the boat, not the outside, that causes the damage.

Let's reflect again[7] on Joshua's conquest of the Promised Land, considering another life lesson that story reveals. It's fascinating how God dealt with Joshua after a terrible loss of troops during a strategic attack of the city of Ai right after the incredible victory at Jericho. The Israelites were brand-new to the conquest of the Promised Land, not yet confident in the Lord's power to protect them and give them victory despite the walls that had fallen down just days before. It was only their second battle, and they were relying on the promise of God that He would fight their battles for them and chase out their enemies.

Joshua spied on the city of Ai and found that he needed to send in only a portion of the troops, about three thousand. Boldly, he sent them in—and they were routed, with thirty-six of his warriors slain on the battlefield in a fight they should have won easily. What had gone wrong? Why did the Lord abandon them? How could they have lost? Guilt, shame, fear, doubt, and insecurity rose up in Joshua, and he fell on his face before God with his clothes torn in lament and dust on his head. God left him there until evening, groveling and questioning the Lord's goodness and provision. And then God spoke:

> *Get up! Why have you fallen on your face? Israel has sinned*; they have transgressed my covenant that I commanded them; they have taken some of the devoted things; they have stolen and lied and put them among their own belongings. *Therefore the people of Israel cannot stand before their enemies.* They turn their backs before their enemies, because they have become devoted for destruction. *I will be with you no more, unless* you destroy the devoted things from among you. *Get up! Consecrate the people.* (Josh. 7:10–13a)

It was then Joshua realized that someone from his army had violated God's command without his knowledge. Upon further examination, it was found that a man named Achan had taken some treasure—some plunder from Jericho—despite God's clear and direct command against it. The conquest of Canaan was not about the Israelites getting wealthy off the land but more about God's judgment on the pagan Canaanites who denied Him. God demanded that certain rules be followed, and any violation of those rules would be given severe consequences.

God was not messing around. He had no patience for Israel complaining about His protection when they weren't holding up their side of the contract. Not even the sweet and honorable heart of Joshua was enough to soften the Lord's response. Twice God told Joshua to get up and then blasted him for the sins of his people.

God is bold. He is strong. He knows that if He stays strong for His people and holds their feet to the fire, they grow stronger. He knows that if He becomes emotional mush, they can't get traction off Him to grow. He knows what He has empowered them to do. He knows what they should know. He's not going to buy in to the whining, complaining, worry, and anxiety if what's fueling it isn't even true. It's not that God isn't compassionate; He is extraordinarily compassionate.[8] But He knows that His strength gives us strength. He will not cave to the pressures and manipulations of the Enemy or sow into anxiety and darkness.

God has provided victory for us, so He will not stand by and watch when we choose defeat. He will not simply comfort us when we're acting on what is false. He wants better for us.

What We Are Accountable For

We are accountable for walking in the victory that God has provided. Therefore,

- because Christ has set us free, we are accountable for letting someone or something enslave us again.[9]
- because God always provides a means of escape from temptation, we are accountable for caving in.[10]
- because the cross means full forgiveness and expresses the unending grace of God, we are accountable for living in shame, guilt, and condemnation.[11]

- because the Lord has provided everything we need for life and godliness, we are accountable for living in a mind-set of scarcity rather than abundance.[12]
- because our inheritances in heaven are secured by the Holy Spirit, we are accountable for losing ourselves in hopelessness and despair.[13]
- because Jesus defeated Satan and rendered his plan void, conquering sin and death, we are accountable for letting ourselves be bullied.[14]

I pray that when you read that list, you feel empowered. The reason we will be held accountable for all these things is because God has given us the victory! We don't have to live lives of fear and worry. We don't have to live in hopelessness. We don't have to live confused and doubting. We don't have to live unhealthily. God has made a way!

Today

Today is our day—the day of salvation.

Today is the day we begin taking back control of our minds and thoughts.

Today is the day we recognize who we are and determine to live as God's children.

Today is the day the Enemy begins to lose control over us.

Today is the day we recognize and realize that we have everything we need to rise above the concerns of this world.

Today is the day we embrace the power, authority, freedom, and strength God has provided to His children.

Today is the day we reverse the vicious cycle of bullying and start to demolish strongholds, storm the gates of hell, and exhibit the self-control Christ died for.

Today is the day we make a strategy to take our promised land, no matter how hard it is.

Today is the day depression loses its grip.

Today is the day anxiety and fear begin to diminish.

Today is the day we order our thoughts and bring them captive.

Today is the day we submit our minds to the Master of all things as an act of offering.

Today is the day we master our minds.

Acknowledgments and Appreciation

This book is dedicated to my beautiful wife, Suzi, and my precious daughters, Jillian and Andie. Thank you for sharing your husband and daddy with the world.

Special thanks goes out to the following people who made this book possible and insightful:

My loving staff and congregation at Bridgeway Christian Church, who live in my heart every day and minister to me as much as I minister to them.

My assistants, Nicole Andrade (LCH Ministries) and Amanda Beck (BCC), who both tell me what to do on a daily basis—and they're always right.

My editor, Karin Buursma, who is a far better writer than I'll ever be.

My agent, Lisa Jackson, who makes working together feel like a fun friendship.

My friend and contributor Jeff Stone, PhD, of Cornerstone Psychological Center.

My personal therapist, Susan Reynolds, MA, MFT, of Valley Psychological Center.

The team at Thomas Nelson Publishing (Joel Kneedler, Lori Cloud, Meaghan Porter), who found time in their busy schedules to not only contribute significantly to this project but also make me feel like I matter.

To my heroes—my mom and dad.

Notes

Foreword

1. John Maxwell, *Thinking for a Change: 11 Ways Highly Successful People Approach Life and Work* (New York: Warner Books, 2003) 27–33.

Chapter 1: The One Thing

1. *City Slickers*, directed by Ron Underwood (1991; Beverly Hills, CA: Twentieth Century Fox, 2015), DVD.
2. Matt. 22:36; Mark 12:28.
3. Gen. 3:22–24.
4. Phil. 3:20.
5. Rom. 8:18–25; 2 Cor. 5:2–4.
6. Luke 22:39–46.
7. Rom. 6:10.
8. Rom. 5:18; 10:4; 1 Cor. 1:30; Phil. 3:9.
9. 2 Cor. 5:17.
10. 2 Peter 1:4.

Chapter 2: Identity Theft

1. "Identity Theft And Cybercrime," Insurance Information Institute, accessed March 27, 2017, http://www.iii.org/fact-statistic/identity -theft-and-cybercrime.

2. Ilana Lowery, "LifeLock CEO shares more than SSN in first 'Reporter's Notebook' event," *Phoenix Business Journal*, February 20, 2014, accessed March 27, 2017, http://www.bizjournals.com /phoenix/news/2014/02/20/lifelock-ceo-shares-more-than-ssn-in .html.

3. Ray Stern, "Cracking LifeLock: Even After a $12 Million Penalty for Deceptive Advertising, the Tempe Company Can't Be Honest About Its Identity-Theft-Protection Service," *Phoenix New Times*, May 13, 2010, accessed March 27, 2017, http://www.phoenixnewtimes .com/news/cracking-lifelock-even-after-a-12-million-penalty-for -deceptive-advertising-the-tempe-company-cant-be-honest-about -its-identity-theft-protection-service-6445863.

4. Cf. Gen. 9:6; 1 Cor. 11:7.

5. Gen. 5:3.

6. See also 2 Cor. 4:4.

7. Col. 3:10; Gen. 1:26–27; Col. 1:15; 2 Cor. 4:4; 1 Cor. 11:7.

8. Ps. 145.

9. Acts 4:24; 1 Tim. 6:15.

10. Ps. 139:1–6, 11–16; Matt. 10:30; John 16:30.

11. Ps. 139:7–10.

12. Isa. 40:28; Rom. 1:25.

13. Deut. 4:31; Ps. 40:11; 1 Chron. 21:13.

14. John 13:25; 10:14; Ex. 29:45.

15. 1 Chron. 16:23–27; Ps. 21:6; 105:43; Isa. 58:14; Luke 10:21; Gal. 5:22; Eccl. 2:24; Ps. 50:7–12.

16. Jer. 9:24; 22:15–16.

17. 2 Sam. 7:28; Ps. 19:7; Rev. 21:5.

18. Ps. 78:38; James 5:11; Neh. 9:17.

19. 1 Cor. 2:9; Ex. 15:11; Gen. 1.

20. Acts 17:24–26.

21. Matt. 3:16.

22. Luke 9:35.

23. 2 Cor. 5:17; Eph. 2:4–5; 5:8.

24. Rom. 15:7; Col. 3:12; 1 Thess. 1:4; 1 John 4:19.

25. John 1:12; Rom. 8:17; Gal. 4:7; Phil. 4:7, 19.

26. Gal. 3:28; Eph. 2:19–22; Phil. 3:20; 1 Cor. 3:16–17; 1 Peter 2:5.

27. Rom. 3:24; 2 Cor. 5:21; Eph. 1:7; 2:13; Col. 2:10.

28. Rom. 8:1; 1 Cor. 1:30; Gal 5:1; Eph. 1:4; 3:12; 4:24.

29. Rom. 8:2; 1 Cor. 1:2; 2 Cor. 3:14.

30. Eph. 1:10–11, 13; 2:6; Col. 3:1–4

31. John 15:1–5; Eph. 1:3; 2:10; 3:6; 5:30.

32. 1 Cor. 3:16; 6:19.

33. Col. 1:21–23.

34. John 8:23; 12:25; 1 Cor. 3:19; 1 John 2:16.

35. John 15:19; 17:16.

36. John 12:31; 14:30; 16:11; 1 Cor. 5:10; 1 John 5:19.

37. John 17:11; Gal. 6:14; Col. 3:2–3; James 1:27; 4:4; 1 John 2:15.

38. Matt. 16:13–20; cf. Mark 8:27–29; Luke 9:18–20.

39. Kenneth Boa, *Conformed to His Image: Biblical and Practical Approaches to Spiritual Formation* (Grand Rapids: Zondervan, 2001), 36.

Chapter 3: The Father of Lies

1. 2 Cor. 2:11.

2. The person we know as the Devil is directly referred to (by popular names) seventy-two times in the Bible: he is referred to thirty-two times as the "Devil," thirty-three times as "Satan," and seven times as "Beelzebub."

3. Isa. 14:12–16; Ezek. 28:12–19.

4. Ezek. 28:14, 16.

5. Ezek. 28:12.

6. 1 Tim. 3:6; Luke 22:31; Ezek. 28:17.

7. Ezek. 16:16–19; Isa. 14:12–19; Rev. 12:4.

8. Heb. 2:7, 9; Dan. 8:17.

9. Job 1:8.

10. Luke 1:19; 1 Peter 1:12; Ezek. 1:4–5, 22–28; Rev. 4:2–11; 5:8–14.

11. John 8:44.

12. John 8:44; 1 John 3:8; 2 Tim. 2:26; 1 Peter 5:8. Taking cues from the mysterious and underdeveloped view of Satan found in the Old Testament (Genesis; Job; Pss. 38:20; 71:13; 109:4, 20, 29; 1 Sam. 29:4; 2 Sam. 19:22; 1 Kings 5:4; 11:14, 23, 25; Num. 22:22, 32; 1 Chron. 21:1) and combining them with the more highly developed view in the New Testament (which leaned heavily upon apocryphal writings during the intertestamental period), we learn quite a bit about what he's like.

13. Gen. 3; Rev. 12:9; Matt. 4:3; 1 Thess. 3:5.

14. Job 1:6–12; 2:1–7; Zech. 3:1, 2.

15. Rev. 12:10; Matt. 4:1.

16. Luke 11:15; 2 Cor. 6:15; Matt. 12:24; 25:41; Eph. 2:2.

17. John 12:31; 14:30; Eph. 2:2; Luke 4:6; Acts 26:18; 2 Cor. 4:4.

18. Mark 4:15; John 8:44; Acts 13:10; Col. 1:13.

19. Rev. 20:2.

20. 1 Peter 5:8.

21. Rev. 9:11.

22. Heb. 2:14.

23. Eph. 6:12.

24. Isa. 27:1.

25. John 17:15; Eph. 6:16; Matt. 6:13.

26. Matt. 4:6; 2 Cor. 2:11; 11:3.

27. 2 Peter 2:11; Heb. 2:7; Ex. 7:11–12; 8:7; Dan. 10:13; Mark 5:2–4; 9:17–26; Acts 19:16; 2 Cor. 10:4–5; Rev. 9:15–19.

28. 2 Cor. 12:7; Luke 13:11, 16; Matt. 10:1; Mark 1:23–26; 3:11; Luke 4:36; Acts 5:16; 8:7; Rev. 16:13.

29. Matt. 8:28; 17:15, 18; Mark 5:15; Luke 8:27–29.

30. Matt. 9:33.

31. Mark 9:25.

32. Matt. 17:15–18.

33. Matt. 12:22.

34. Mark 9:22.

35. Mark 9:18.

36. Luke 13:11.

37. Rev. 9:3–4.

38. 1 Sam. 16:14; 18:10; 19:9.

39. John 14:30; 1 Tim. 4:1; Rev. 2:9, 24; Rev. 9:16; Dan. 10:13, 20. He's not only the prior master of this world (before the cross) and the current dominator worldwide, but also he has significant territories that he rules intensely through either personal presence or through his demonic leadership.

40. 2 Peter 2:10–13; Jude 8–11; Acts 18:11–20.

41. Ps. 78:49; Eph. 6:12; Rev. 12:7–9; Luke 4:6; Job 1:12; 2:6; 1 Cor. 10:13; 1 Peter 1:12; Rev. 20:2, 7.

42. James 2:19.

43. 1 John 4:4; 1 Cor. 6:19; 2 Tim. 1:14; John 14:17; 1 John 2:14; Luke 8:28; James 2:19; 2 Peter 2:4; Jude 6; Rev. 9:14.

44. 1 John 3:8; Heb. 2:14.

45. John 16:11.

46. Matt. 13:36–43; Rom. 16:20; Rev. 20:2; Luke 10:18; John 12:31; Rev. 12.

47. Col. 2:15; John 12:31; Rev. 12:11; Titus 2:14; Col. 1:13; Rev. 3:21.

48. 2 Thess. 3:3; James 4:7; Rev. 2:24.

49. 1 Cor. 6:3.

50. Rom. 16:20; Rev. 12–20; Matt. 25:41; 2 Peter 2:4; Jude 6; John 12:31; Luke 10:18; John 16:11; Col. 2:15; Rom. 8:38–39; Rev. 12:11; 1 John 2:8, 13–14; Rev. 17:14; 1 Tim. 3:6; Rev. 20:1–3, 10.

51. Rev. 12:12.

52. 1 Peter 5:8; Luke 13:16.

53. Matt. 16:23; Mark 4:15; 1 Thess. 2:18.

54. Luke 8:27; Eph. 2:12; 4:18; Col. 1:21.

55. 2 Tim. 2:26.

56. Eph. 6:11; 1 Tim. 3:7; 2 Tim. 2:26.

57. Luke 10:41–42.

58. Luke 22:31.

59. 1 Cor. 1:10–13; John 9:16; Rom. 16:17; 1 Cor. 11:18; Judg. 9:23–25; Rev. 16:13–14; Titus 3:10; Jude 19.

60. *Merriam-Webster*, s.v. "lie," accessed March 5, 2017, https://www .merriam-webster.com/dictionary/lie.

61. Gen. 3:4–5.

62. Rev. 3:9; Acts 5:3; 2 Cor. 11:10–15.

63. *Merriam-Webster*, s.v. "counterfeit," accessed March 5, 2017, https://www.merriam-webster.com/dictionary/counterfeit.

64. 2 Thess. 2:9–10; Ex. 7:11–12, 22; Deut. 13:1–2; Matt. 24:24; Mark 13:22; Rev. 13:13–14; 19:20.

65. Rev. 13:2; 16:13.

66. Ex. 3–12.

67. Ex. 7:8–12.

68. 1 Cor. 5:5; Judg. 9:23; 1 Tim. 1:20; Ps. 78:49; 2 Cor. 12:7; 1 Kings 22:19–23; 1 Sam. 16:14; Rev. 16:13–16.

69. Gen. 22:1–19; Job 1–2; Matt. 4:1; 1 Cor. 7:5; 1 Peter 1:3–9.

70. "The Hebrew word *nasah* and the Greek word *peirazō* both carry a broad range of meaning that allows them to be translated as either 'temptation' or 'testing' in the Bible. In the first instance, the word implies enticement to do evil, while, in the second, the connotation is an event or process that proves one's character or determines the depth or integrity of one's commitment to God." In Mark Allan Powell, ed., *HarperCollins Bible Dictionary, Revised and Updated* (New York: HarperCollins, 2011), 1027.

71. Ps. 5:4; James 1:13; 3 John 11.

72. Gen. 49:25; Deut. 33:26; 2 Chron. 14:11; 32:8; Pss. 18:6; 40:17; 46:1; Acts 26:22; 1 Peter 1:5.

73. Luke 22:31; Heb. 2:14; John 14:30; Matt. 12:28; Luke 13:16; Acts 10:38; Gal. 1:4; Eph. 1:19–22; Rom. 8:38–39; Eph. 3:10; Col. 1:16; 2:10, 15; Luke 13:32; 4:18; Matt. 8:16, 31–32; Mark 1:32–34; 5:12–13; Luke 4:40–41; 8:32–33; Matt. 4:24; Mark 1:23–26; Luke 4:33–35; Mark 1:39; Matt. 15:22–28; Mark 7:25–30; Matt. 17:18; Mark 9:25; Luke 9:42; Mark 1:25; Luke 4:35, 41.

74. Mark 1:8; 13:11; John 14:26; Acts 1:8; 4:8; 5:3; 7:55; 10:38; Eph. 4:30; 1 Thess. 1:5; 2 Tim. 1:14; Heb. 2:4.

75. Jude 9; Matt. 4:6; 18:10; Luke 22:43; Acts 5:19; 12:7–15; Heb. 13:2.

76. Acts 1:8; 6:8; Rom. 15:19; 1 Cor. 4:20; 12:6, 11; 2 Cor. 6:3–7; 10:4–6; Eph. 3:7; 1 Thess. 1:5; 2 Thess. 1:11.

77. Eph. 1:15–21; 2 Peter 1:3; Rom. 1:20.

Chapter 4: Temptation ~~Island~~ Desert

1. Matt. 18:7.
2. Cf. Hos. 4:12.
3. 2 Tim. 3:5–7; Titus 3:3–7.
4. 1 Thess. 3:5.
5. Cf. Isa. 53:3–4; Mark 14:38.
6. The verse that Jesus quotes was from Deuteronomy 8:2–3, which explicitly states that God caused the Israelites to hunger. It was on purpose. Being hungry was the test. To complain about a test of obedience is to fail the test. To wiggle out of the test and satisfy the necessary craving another way is to fail the test.
7. John 12:31; 2 Cor. 4:4; Eph. 2:2.
8. Jesus' reply to Satan doesn't seem to fit as nicely with a temptation of approval, though. His response was rather direct: "You shall not put the Lord your God to the test" (Matt. 4:7). Clearly, the temptation involved trying to manipulate or push God to do something that He may not have wanted to do at that moment.
9. Job 38:1–4; 40:7–8; 42:1–3. One of the struggles with reading the book of Job is that we all realize that we would have asked why and complained about our treatment too. But God still corrected Job and reminded him that he didn't have the right to make demands of God.
10. Heb. 5:8–9; cf. Luke 24:26; Rom. 5:3; 2 Cor. 12:9; 1 Peter 2:21.
11. Notice that Luke puts the genealogy link of Christ and Adam in between the baptism and the temptation in his gospel.

Chapter 5: Arming the Resistance

1. Luke 22:31–32; John 13:2.
2. Acts 5:3.
3. 1 Cor. 10:13.
4. Heb. 4:15.
5. 1 John 4:9–10; Eph. 2:4; John 15:13; Rom. 5:8.
6. John 19:30.
7. Col. 1:13.

8. Col. 2:15.

9. 1 Cor. 15:25; Heb. 10:12–13.

10. 1 Sam. 12:16; Eph. 6:11.

11. 2 Thess. 3:3; Phil. 4:5–7; 2 Tim. 1:12–14; 1 Peter 1:5.

12. 1 Tim. 6:20; 2 Cor. 2:11; Eph. 6:11; James 4:7; 1 Peter 5:9.

13. Cf. Gal. 5:1; Phil. 4:1; 2 Thess. 2:15.

14. John 17:15; Matt. 6:13; Luke 22:31–32; Eph. 6:11, 18.

15. Phil. 2:10; Isa. 45:23; Ps. 118:10–12; Mark 16:17–18; Luke 10:17; Acts 16:18.

16. 1 John 4:4.

17. 2 Peter 1:3.

18. Prov. 5:22–23; 20:1.

19. Luke 11:2–4.

20. Matt. 26:41; Gal. 6:1; Luke 21:8.

21. Prov. 16:18; 1 Cor. 10:12; Isa. 47:10–11.

Chapter 6: Making Monsters

1. *Merriam-Webster*, s.v. "slavery," accessed March 5, 2017, https://www.merriam-webster.com/dictionary/slavery.

2. *Pinocchio*, directed by Ben Sharpsteen and Hamilton Luske (1940; Burbank, CA: Buena Vista, 1999), DVD.

3. 2 Cor. 4:2; Rom. 2:15.

4. 1 Cor. 8:7–12; 10:25–29.

5. 2 Tim. 1:3.

6. Rom. 9:1; Acts 23:1; 24:16; 2 Cor. 1:12; 5:11.

7. Heb. 9:9–14; 1 Peter 3:21; 1 Tim. 3:9.

8. 1 Tim. 1:5, 19; Heb. 13:18; 1 Peter 3:16.

9. Prov. 3:5–6.

Chapter 7: Hostile Takeover

1. *Merriam-Webster*, s.v. "depression," accessed March 8, 2017, https://www.merriam-webster.com/dictionary/depression.

2. Matt. 6.

3. Lance Hahn, *How to Live in Fear: Mastering the Art of Freaking Out* (Nashville: Thomas Nelson, 2016), 141–56.

4. Josh. 6; 2 Chron. 20:22; 2 Sam. 6:14–23; 1 Chron. 5:20.

5. Rom. 1:25.

6. 2 Sam 7:25–26; Pss. 34:3; 69:30; Luke 1:46–47.

7. That includes street drugs, steroids, and prescription medication taken other than as intended. It's a fine line when we get into pharmaceutical drugs, but the result of abuse is the same. Whether someone is hooked on oxycodone, Vicodin, or heroin, the body goes through a process of ingestion, adjustment, reliance, and detoxification.

8. I say that as a proponent of the appropriate use of alcohol, even as a pastor. I am not afraid of alcohol, but I am afraid of foolish people. I think that alcohol is a neutral that was designed by God as a blessing to mankind, but we ruin it. In fact, I think we are fairly good at ruining most of God's blessings with distortion.

9. Despite the resurgence of vaping, hookah, flavored cigarettes, cloves, and electronic cigs, smoking isn't what it used to be.

10. Pornography is the new designer drug for men. Pornography has been around since the ancient world, but the proliferation, the tailoring, the niche, the intensity, and the creativity today have taken it to a whole new level. I cannot confidently name one man I have met, inside or outside the church, who has not struggled with pornography. In my experience, almost 100 percent of men have been tempted, which is far higher than any other addiction ratio I've come across.

11. 1 Cor. 9.27, 1 Thess. 4.4, 2 Tim. 3.3.

12. James Olds, "Pleasure centers in the brain," *Scientific American*, October 1956, https://www.scientificamerican.com/article/pleasure-centers-in-the-brain.

13. William E. Cohen and Darryl S. Inaba, *Uppers, Downers, All-Arounders*, 7th ed. (Medford, OR: CNS, 2011).

14. Josh. 6:1–21.

15. Josh. 7:1–26.

16. Josh. 23:13.

Chapter 8: The Land of Make-Believe

1. "How to Make a Horror Film," *WikiHow*, accessed March 27, 2017, http://www.wikihow.com/make-a-horror-film.
2. Cf. Col. 2:18–19.

Chapter 9: All Hail the King

1. 1 Peter 2:16; Rev. 22:3.
2. John 15:15; Heb. 9:26.
3. 2 Peter 2:1.
4. Matt. 12:30.
5. John 1:29; 2 Cor. 5:19; 1 John 2:2.
6. Luke 16:13.
7. Gal. 3:22.
8. Ps. 139:13.
9. 1 Cor. 7:23.
10. Matt. 24:45–51; Luke 12:35–48; 17:7–10; 19:11–27; John 12:26; 18:36; Acts 4:29–30; Rom. 1:1; 14:4; 1 Cor. 4:1; 2 Cor. 6:4; Gal. 1:10; Eph. 3:7; 6:21; Phil. 1:1; Col. 1:23–25; 2 Tim. 2:24; Titus 1:1; James 1:1; 2 Peter 1:1; Jude 1; Rev. 1:1; 6:11; 19:2–5.
11. Eph. 4:1; 2 Thess. 1:11.
12. US Department of State, "What Is a U.S. Embassy?" Discover Diplomacy, accessed February 17, 2017, https://diplomacy.state.gov /discoverdiplomacy/diplomacy101/places/170537.htm.
13. Luke 16:13; James 1:5–8; Ps. 119:113; James 3:11; Matt. 16:21–23.
14. Matt. 12:30; 1 John 3:6.
15. 1 Sam. 2:34–35.
16. God did tremendous work to get the Hebrews to start thinking outside of a slave mind-set. (They were slaves to Egypt for more than four hundred years.)
17. Rom. 12:1.
18. Phil. 4:8; 2 Cor. 10:5; Rom. 1:21, 28; 12:3; 13:14; 1 Cor. 10:12; 14:20; Gal. 6:3; Eph. 4:17; 1 Tim. 6:5; James 1:7-8; 1 Peter 1:13; 4:7.
19. Isa. 55:8–9; Ps. 92:5.
20. Num. 23:19; Deut. 7:9; Ps. 110:4; Jer. 30:24; Heb. 7:21.

21. John 3:16; Rom. 8:39; Ex. 34:6; Gen. 24:27; 1 Kings 8:23; Neh. 13:22; John 16:27; Rom. 1:7; 15:30.

22. Gal. 5:22–23; 2 Cor. 13:11.

23. Deut. 31:6; Job 38; Pss. 33:8; 89:6–7; 118:6.

24. Gal. 3:8.

25. 2 Cor. 11:31.

26. Luke 19:41.

27. John 11:33.

28. Acts 2:31-33; 5:31; Heb. 10:12.

29. Eph. 1:3–10.

30. Acts 14:1–4.

31. Ps. 4:3; Ex. 8:22; Deut. 10:8; 1 Chron. 23:13.

32. Luke 24:44–45; 2 Cor. 3:14–16.

33. Job 38:36.

34. Matt. 10:30.

35. Heb. 4:12–13; Ezek. 11:5; Rev. 2:23.

36. Ps. 139:4.

37. Cf. 1 Chron. 28:9; 29:17; Pss. 7:9; 17:3; 26:2; Prov. 17:3; Jer. 12:3; 20:12; 1 Thess. 2:4.

38. Cf. Deut. 13:3; 2 Chron. 32:31; Jer. 11:20; Heb. 3:8.

39. Ps. 94:11.

40. Ps. 139:2.

41. Ex. 13:17–18.

42. Eph. 6:13.

43. Eph. 4:3.

44. Eph. 6:16.

45. Mark 5:15.

46. James 4:7.

47. Prov. 9:9.

48. Ps. 119:27.

49. 2 Thess. 1:12; Rom. 8:17, 30.

Chapter 10: Replacement Therapy

1. Harvard-Smithsonian Center for Astrophysics, "Event Horizon Telescope Reveals Magnetic Fields at Milky Way's Central Black Hole," *ScienceDaily,* December 3, 2015, www.sciencedaily.com /releases/2015/12/151203150233.htm.
2. Rom. 6:6; Eph. 4:22; Col. 3:9.
3. John 4:10; 7:37–39.
4. Cf. Eph. 4:17–5:20.
5. 1 Kings 8:47–48; 2 Chron. 6:37–38; Jonah 3:6.
6. Ezek. 14:6.
7. Cf. Ps. 78:34; Isa. 1:27; Jer. 34:15; Matt. 11:20.
8. Cf. 1 Kings 8:48–51; Matt. 21:28–32; 27:3–5.
9. Phil. 3:19–21.
10. Cf. Eph. 4:17–21.
11. 1 Chron. 22:17–19; Titus 1:7–9.
12. Matt. 13:1–9, 18–23.
13. A more easily understandable teaching on this subject is available from John Ortberg's book *The Life You've Always Wanted*, which he lovingly describes as "Dallas Willard for Dummies."
14. Matt. 4:1–11; Luke 4:1–13.
15. Matt. 14:13; Mark 3:7; Luke 9:10; 22:41. The discipline of silence is not only being away from noise, but also being silent ourselves and listening more than talking.
16. Matt. 6:3.
17. Luke 6:12; 9:18, 28; 11:1; 18:1–8.
18. Kenneth Boa, *Conformed to His Image: Biblical and Practical Approaches to Spiritual Formation* (Grand Rapids, MI: Zondervan, 2001), 78–79.
19. Eph. 2:6.
20. Phil. 3:20.
21. Eph. 1:3; 1 Peter 3:22.
22. 2 Cor. 5:7.
23. Cf. Pss. 13:2; 25:1.
24. Cf. Pss. 103:22; 104:1, 35; 146:1.
25. Ps. 49:3; 2 Peter 1:12–13.

26. 2 Cor. 10:7.
27. Pss. 1:2; 19:14; 119:15.
28. Gal. 5:1.
29. Phil. 4:7.
30. Eph. 4:13.

Chapter 11: Who's the Boss?

1. Gen. 1–2.
2. Matt. 21:33–41; 25:14–30.
3. James 4:8 10.
4. Cf. 2 Tim. 4:3–5; Titus 2:2; 1 Peter 4:7; 5:8; 2 Thess. 2:1–2.
5. Dallas Willard, *The Spirit of the Disciplines: Understanding How God Changes Lives* (New York: HarperCollins, 1999).
6. James 5:17.
7. In chapter 7 I made the point that the Israelites cleared the land piece by piece, little by little, so they could take it all and hold it.
8. Ex. 22:27; 34:6–7; Ps. 78:38; James 5:11.
9. Gal. 5:1.
10. 1 Cor. 10:13.
11. Eph. 1:7; 2:13; Col. 2:14; Acts 10:43; Rom. 4:7; Heb. 10:18; 1 John 1:9; 2:12; Rom. 5:2.
12. 2 Peter 1:3; 1 Tim. 6:6; Eph. 1:15–23.
13. Eph. 1:11–14; Rom. 5:1–5; 8:25; 12:12; 1 Cor. 15:19–20; 2 Cor. 1:10; 3:12; Col. 1:5.
14. Luke 10:19; 2 Tim. 1:7; 1 Cor. 15:25–26; Rev. 12:7–8; Heb. 2:15; 13:6.

About the Author

Lance Hahn is the senior pastor of Bridgeway Christian Church in Rocklin, California. He loves reading and teaching God's Word. In his first book, *How to Live in Fear: Mastering the Art of Freaking Out*, he shared personal stories about his struggles with anxiety, offered tools for thriving through fear, and guided fellow sufferers into a life of faith and trust in a God who has not forgotten them.

Outside of leading Bridgeway and uniting churches in the Sacramento region, Lance is a popular speaker, a movie buff, and a collecting nerd who loves to write articles, blogs, and books in his spare time. Lance is married to his wonderful wife, Suzi. They have two incredible daughters, and they round out their home with a tri-colored Cavalier King Charles Spaniel named Bella.

Find freedom in an age of anxiety

How to Live in Fear

Mastering the Art of **Freaking Out**

Lance Hahn